D1083352

BANKING ON TRADITION

The 130-Year History of the
Frost National Bank

MAIN PLAZA, CIRCA 1868. *This five-by-eight foot painting by José Vives-Atsara, dated 1965, hangs in the Frost Motor Bank lower level. It depicts the mercantile store (at right) from which Colonel T. C. Frost began his banking operation in 1868. The original San Fernando Cathedral, not yet reconstructed, stands across the unsurfaced street from the store.*

Banking on Tradition

THE 130-YEAR HISTORY OF THE
FROST NATIONAL BANK

by Tom Walker

Banking on Tradition
The 130-Year History of the Frost National Bank

by Tom Walker

First Edition, 2000

LIBRARY OF CONGRESS CATALOG CARD NUMBER 00-130203

INTERNATIONAL STANDARD BOOK NUMBER 0-9678670-0-2

✦ ✦ ✦

Man's chief purpose is the creation and preservation
of values: that is what gives meaning to our civilization.
And the participation in this is what gives significance,
ultimately, to the individual human life.

— Lewis Mumford
Faith for Living, 1940

contents

foreword

What follows in the pages ahead is the history of an organization that has not just endured for over 130 years but, throughout them, stood fast to the values personified by its founder. It is the story of how since its founding, that institution–the Frost National Bank–has remained intimately intertwined with the interests of the people it serves. Engendering long-term relationships between those who labor and those whom their labor serves is the hallmark of this bank's existence.

For many years now, I have been a student, observer, chronicler, historian, and media reporter of Texas history–San Antonio history in particular. I first became closely associated with the Frost family in the 1970s, when Tom Frost Jr. volunteered to host the Mexican-American Friendship Council, of which I had been president since 1955. During my long association, I have seen few businesses so closely woven into the fabric of their communities as the Frost National Bank.

That closeness was the aim of its founder, Colonel T. C. Frost, on the day in 1868 when he began the operation that would become the Frost National Bank in a corner of the one-room country store he operated on San Antonio's Main Plaza. Colonel Frost had come to Texas from Tennessee in 1854 as a young Latin professor at Austin College in Huntsville. He migrated from teacher to lawyer to public servant, Texas

Ranger, Confederate soldier, freight operator, and merchant before starting up what is today the largest commercial bank headquartered in Texas.

By forging associations with partners who espouse the same principles of integrity and service to the community, the Frost National Bank now reaches not just major segments of Texas but across the border into Mexico. Like San Antonio itself, this bank has always had a special relationship with Mexico. That's why it was a staunch and early supporter of NAFTA. And in 1994, its efforts to help locate the prestigious NADBank (North American Development Bank) in the Alamo City were successful as well.

The values by which Colonel Frost lived, and which created his success, are the same values embraced today by the fifth generation now in management roles within this multibillion-dollar enterprise. More than anything else, those values enabled the bank to weather the two fiercest storms in its history: the Great Depression of the 1930s and the Texas banking disaster of the 1980s.

I salute all who, since its 1868 inception, have contributed to the achievements of this institution. As a citizen of Texas, I look forward to Frost Bank's carrying its proud heritage into the 21st Century and the new Millennium.

Henry Guerra
November 17, 1999
San Antonio, Texas

synopsis

The First Hundred Years: 1868 Through 1967

To commemorate Frost Bank's 130th anniversary in 1998, the chapters ahead chronicle events that occurred during the 30 years since the first volume of Frost history, *A Century on Main Plaza*, appeared in 1968, the bank's centennial.

First, however, it seems worthwhile to glance back upon the colorful characters and exciting events of those first hundred years, recorded in that earlier volume. It will become apparent, as one reads this newer book, how faithfully the fourth and fifth generations of Frost management have adhered, over the past 30 years, to the old-fashioned philosophy, values, and ethos promulgated by the first three.

Certainly that was a remarkable feat. Those 30 years witnessed a whirlwind of unsettling change in virtually every American industry, banking included. Being old-fashioned in any respect was not in style. Too often, sadly, tried-and-true conservative tradition yielded to the demands of expediency, trendiness, rapid growth, and quick profits.

But at Frost Bank, thanks to a stubborn refusal to "reevaluate" values or restructure traditional priorities, philosophical continuity was preserved even as the bank radically changed, as it had to, with the times in size, scope, organization, geography, technology, and services. A contention of this book is that Frost Bank endured, and ultimately prevailed, in an era of industry tumult and reversal of fortune because it preserved such continuity.

A second conviction holds that one key to that preservation was the bank's orderly succession of management, itself an example of dogged continuity. For most banks, the era ushered in a revolving-door syndrome of "stable growth" managers periodically being replaced by "turnaround" or "crisis management" teams, themselves replaced by new teams of stable growth managers once the crises passed. As with the major league baseball clubs of today, the only constant was change and the only faces one could count on seeing year after year were new faces. At Frost Bank, however, the team was perennially stable and dependable, like the New York Yankees of the Fifties. Despite the times, the organization has been loyal to the players, the players to the organization, and the customers, therefore, to the bank itself.

A third theme recurring in the chapters ahead is the dynamic synergy that has always existed between Frost Bank and its community. Galvanized by that dynamic, their fortunes have paralleled one another. Since its founding during the lean and hungry days of Reconstruction, the bank has sought to nurture and develop the crossroads community growing up around it and with it. That crossroads community eventually became a great city, the nation's eighth largest.

The San Antonio community is Frost Bank's "home court" and always will be. But this book also illustrates the bank's efforts to be a good corporate citizen in the other communities to which it expanded. Galveston and Corpus Christi are prime examples. "Our reason for being," more than one Frost Bank CEO has stated, "is not only to make money for our stockholders but to provide a productive service to society and the community." It has the ring of corporate rhetoric, but history has confirmed that they meant what they said.

That quote introduces another, related theme to be sounded in the forthcoming chapters: the bank's predominant image of itself as an instrument to be used for the betterment of people rather than for the success of projects or accumulation of profits. "We're not in the money business," the storied Joseph Hardin ("Mr. Joe") Frost, the bank's third president, never tired of reminding his junior officers. "We're in the people business. We don't make loans to businesses, we make loans to people—to build long-term relationships."

Finally, the chapters ahead illustrate the bank's stubborn resiliency, its ability to suffer slings and arrows of outrageous fortune yet emerge from such misfortunes, as broken bones are said to heal, stronger than before. The sheer ability to survive has been an ingredient in its recipe for success, and the yeasts of that recipe have been sound assets, high liquidity, solid reserves through thick and thin, and the effort to be the best, rather than the biggest, even in the decades of its most dramatic growth.

Now onto that capsule history, a synopsis of those first hundred years—the first three generations of Frost leadership—chronicled in *A Century on Main Plaza.*

THE FIRST GENERATION: Colonel Thomas Claiborne "T. C." Frost (1833–1903)

Frost Bank's conservative tradition and old-fashioned company values are the philosophical legacy of its founder-patriarch, Colonel Thomas Claiborne ("T. C.") Frost. Rarely in the history of American industry has one man still exerted so potent an influence on an enterprise 130 years after founding it.

History records the Colonel as an heroic figure, gifted with protean talents and prodigious drive. He could have excelled, and did in fact excel, at so many undertakings that his ultimate career as a banker seems fated by destiny. He was that rarest of men, a scholar blessed with an innate love of books and classical learning but also with uncanny business acumen and common horse sense. Miraculously, within his psyche, the idealistic scholar and tough-minded businessman did not conflict but complemented each other, and the result was the sort of individual about whom legends are woven.

A Tennessee-educated Alabama native, Colonel Frost came to Texas in 1854 to teach Latin at Austin College, then in Huntsville. There, he learned to read the law, at night, under the tutelage of Judge Henderson Yoakum, legal counsel to the great Sam Houston. The hats young T. C. Frost would wear with style and distinction before becoming the best banker south of the Mason-Dixon line were not just those of educator and lawyer but Confederate colonel, Texas Ranger, merchant, auctioneer, freight line operator, postmaster, real estate dealer, and district attorney of Comanche County.

His remarkable knack for changing vocations bespoke not just handy versatility but a remarkable flexibility: The Colonel could adapt to virtually any adverse situation. "Institutions, like people, are largely products of their heritage," goes an old adage, and the bank T. C. Frost would father was to inherit such flexibility, such adaptability, from him. This inheritance endowed it with the ability to change when the times demanded, adjust to circumstances rather than demand that they adjust, swim with the tide of history rather than against it.

In 1865, the Colonel returned home from a national crisis, the Civil War. It was the vindictive era of a new crisis—Reconstruction— and he found himself barred from practicing law because he had been a Confederate officer. But like the bank he was to found, the Colonel was at his best in times of crisis: They tested his mettle—he was nothing if not a survivor. Trying on another hat, he achieved instant success by operating a horse-and-wagon freight operation between San Antonio and Indianola, the Calhoun County port in Matagorda Bay.

Two years later, he sold his business and plunged $3000 into a partnership to rescue the sinking fortunes of his brother John Morrison Frost's mercantile and auctioneering enterprise. Clearly, the Colonel was a risk taker. But his Midas touch combined with his voracious appetite for hard work were a surefire formula for success. Within the year, the resuscitated business (in a one-story structure on dust-blown Main Plaza) was turning a profit. Within 10 years, it was one of the state's fastest-growing mercantile operations.

Colonel Frost foresaw Texas growing as fast as his little partnership had if new arrivals were supplied with the farm implements, guns and ammunition, boots and hats and work clothes, harnesses and saddles and buggies and other wares they needed to survive on the frontier. He lent his own capital to these families seeking a new life; he stocked goods, mainly wool, for them until the market was favorable for sale; he even made loans on the stock he was holding. Effectively, he was functioning as a banker—a loan officer, a financial manager—before he ever founded a bank. In due time, his profits allowed him to convert a corner of his one-room country store into a makeshift bank and provide money and credit to the settlers.

Such efforts, which entailed risk, established a tradition that became inseparable from his bank's identity: the rendering of community service. The Colonel served the crossroads community, San Antonio, he worked to create. He had entered a business to help his brother get back on his feet. Now he was helping his fellow Texans stay on theirs—and developing the quadrant of the state soon to be known as South Texas. He was also doing all right for himself. But he cared more about his relationship with those Texans, and with the struggling frontier community, than about profits, which he would have reaped from any business he grew.

This caring, that priority, would give rise to the Frost hallmark known as "relationship banking." Anecdotes illustrating it are legion: One has it that the Colonel was occasionally given to evenings of sitting in his backyard and staring up at the sky. Once, asked by his daughter

Lucie why he did that, he replied, "It hasn't rained for such a long time, and my customers are worried about the drouth."

This man valued integrity as the quintessence of character and a sound credit rating as the evidence of a businessperson's character. A letter he wrote from New York to his wife, dated February 26, 1887, contains the following paragraph:

I had Mr. North request one of the large houses here to procure from Dunn Mercantile Agency a confidential statement of the standing and credit of T. C. Frost—a copy of which I enclose you. When we consider that there is no advertising, no political puffing, no flattery in the statement but a confidential expression, in a business way, from which men make credits, it becomes something to be very proud of, and it is a great pleasure to have our children know in later life that I had earned such a position in the business world. Nothing will do them more good or appeal more strongly to their pride. Preserve it for our children.

The credit statement to which he refers, issued from the Office of R. G.. Dunn & Co., New York, N.Y., read:

Statement in detail:
T. C. Frost, San Antonio, Texas. In business for the last 18 years and added a banking business a few years ago. Has been a successful business man. His trade lies largely with ranch men in this section, which necessitates giving long credits, which is profitable as he is a good collector. With a complete knowledge of this class of trade he has made money by it. Stock $50,000. Owns valuable real estate in this city and it is worth $150,000—clear. Keeps his affairs in good shape, is in excellent condition and in high credit.

The statement was glowing praise, written in an era when banks outside the Northeast were being called "mad, untamable beasts." Yet the Colonel's one-room country-store bank, solid as the Rock of Ages, continued to thrive as the "untamable beasts" were felled by circumstance. In the 1890s, the decade of a severe national depression, his bank fared well enough to buy another bank and even take on partners: In 1892, it acquired Thornton, Wright & Company, formerly the Traders National Bank, taking over deposit accounts and assets (including real estate) to offset deposit liability. And in 1894, to beef up management, the Colonel and his bank took on two partners.

One partner, J. P. Barclay, had worked for him years earlier and impressed him as a man of promise; the other, J. T. Woodhull, was the Colonel's son-in-law and longtime cashier. The partnership, T. C. Frost & Company, demonstrated not only Colonel Frost's unshakable confidence in his bank but also his faith in the nation. Both were justified. The bank emerged from the depression stronger than ever. In so doing, it defined itself to the world as a survivor and established a precedent for future crises.

On its 19th Century voyage, the bank erected community milestones: its first telephone system, installed in 1882; its first newspaper ad, published in 1887; its first electric lights (replacing gas fixtures), beaming in 1888. Its biggest step was taken in 1899, when the bank was granted the charter it had applied for under the National Banking Act. That meant that T. C. Frost & Company, Bankers, a private concern in a provincial hinterland, would enter the 20th Century as the Frost National Bank and be allowed to issue currency. At the turn of the century, the step from operating a private bank to a national one was a quantum leap. Hereafter, Frost Bank would be a player in the history of not just regional or state but national banking. Its eye was on the future, and that too would become a Frost Bank tradition. With a new century at hand, it was moving not just with the times but ahead of them.

No other American bank had come so far, so fast, from such humble beginnings. Conceivably, the bank was a success *because* its founder was a neophyte, an amateur, a maverick in the field. Not knowing any other, the Colonel did things his own way, which turned out to be the right way for the time and place. It may have been fortunate that he was not a creature of the banking industry, schooled in its bad habits and blind orthodoxies. The truth, in fact, was the reverse. The Colonel's banking industry was his own creation, a product of his intelligence, persona, vision, and business acumen. He imbued his bank with his identity.

An apt eulogy to the Colonel and his bank appeared in the *Texas Stockman and Farmer* magazine of San Antonio a few days after his death, in November 1903. It read in part: "It is almost safe to say that no man in Texas was better or more favorably known to the commercial world than was Colonel Frost. With his wonderful brain power, energy and the hardest kind of work, he succeeded in building up, in the Frost National Bank, one of the greatest financial institutions in the state, which will no doubt exist for many years to come, a monument to his wonderful ability as a financier."

Honesty and integrity. Never breaking his word. Genuinely caring about his fellow man. Taking pride in his credit rating. Protecting the confidentiality of his customers and treasuring their trust in him while being cautious and conservative in his reports to them. Cherishing his relationship with them, and with the community. Keeping his bank's assets sound, its liquidity high, its customers' deposits secure. Putting quality service over profit and growth because he believed the latter two would issue spontaneously from the first. Pious though it sounds, such priorities constituted this patriarch's legacy. When Colonel T. C. Frost died, the torch of that legacy was passed to his family as tradition. What had worked in the 19th Century, counseled the voice of that tradition, would work in the 20th Century, because values are timeless.

THE SECOND GENERATION: T. C. Frost Jr. (1879–1940) and
Joseph Hardin "Mr. Joe" Frost (1881–1956)

Colonel T. C. Frost fathered three sons. Upon his death, the eldest, 24-year-old T. C. Frost Jr., succeeded him as bank president. The two younger Frost brothers, Joseph Hardin and John, were working in the bank also.

Physically robust, a sailing buff, a smart poker player and a lucky one, the new president knew he had big shoes to fill. He welcomed the challenge with confidence and vigor. He faced his first major crisis, four years into his presidency, with the national Panic of 1907. A disastrous concentration of U. S. capital reserves in Manhattan banks, coupled with an overvaluation of copper stocks, had triggered a run on those banks. A nationwide capital shortage and panic ensued.

At Frost National Bank, T. C. Frost Jr. confronted the crisis, calmly and squarely, with the aid of a Clearing House Association he presciently had organized two years earlier, with himself at its helm. The Association created a tightly knit coordination among local banks by standardizing policies and procedures and making daily settlements of checks each bank received for deposit on the others. When the Panic of 1907 struck, one insolvent San Antonio bank failed. Thanks to the Clearing House Association, however, Frost and the other member banks had cash enough on hand to cover withdrawals. Before 1908 dawned, public confidence in the local money supply had been restored, the panic forestalled.

It was a dramatic victory for the young bank president, and established his reputation as an astute businessman with the foresight of his celebrated father. It also established consumer confidence in the bank for generations to follow. In the decades ahead, foresight—the ability to anticipate trouble and confront it preemptively—would become another hallmark of the bank and save it from disasters as improvident banks toppled all around. In the tradition of his father, T. C. Frost Jr. valued integrity more than profits and making money for his customers more than making money off them.

T. C. Frost Jr.'s presidency has been underrated, occurring as it did between those of two legends: his father and his brother Joe. Actually, the bank made bold, headlong strides during his tenure. In 1910, it hired its first female employee. In 1914, it instituted customer statement-posting machines, which replaced hand posting. A few months later, it constructed a two-story office building on Main Plaza to adjoin its existing quarters.

Nineteen-fourteen was also the year Dallas won the coveted location for the district's Federal Reserve Bank. The Federal Reserve Banking System had been created to provide services to member banks and to supply a stable flow of currency for the country. Frost National was one of five banks in the district to execute the organizational certificate incorporating the new Federal Reserve Bank of Dallas. On May 18, 1914, at Dallas's Adolphus Hotel, T. C. Frost Jr. signed for the Frost National Bank as an incorporator. It would prove the first step in the proud tradition of Frost relationship with the "Fed" which continues today.

In 1921, with a Colonel-like eye to the future, Frost Bank issued 5000 shares of stock for a new 12-story bank building—the city's tallest and first to circulate fresh air—at the corner of Main and Commerce. (Half-a-block north of it, at Main and Flores, had stood the old warehouse where the Colonel once stored wool for his customers.) The building officially opened in 1922. The construction cost $800,000—and decorating, new equipment, and furnishings ran $300,000 more. It was a lot of money at the time. But it provided a gracious home for the bank over the next 50 years, a grand building in which the Colonel's spirit could be felt as a hovering presence. And it now provides a meeting place for the City Council every Thursday.

T. C. Frost Jr. may have made his boldest move in 1920, when he invited "outsiders"—prominent local businessmen he knew and trusted—to acquire Frost stock and serve on the Board as directors. (Previously, such honors were reserved for Frost family members and bank officers.) At the same time, he initiated the tradition of annual reports to stockholders, and furthered the Frost tradition of reaching out to the world with careful, considered expansiveness. This reaching out bespoke a growing flexibility, demonstrating that the bank was willing to change before change was thrust upon it. It was reminiscent of the Colonel, who had bravely opened the bank's doors to partners in the middle of a depression.

During this period, the bank had to navigate the treacherous waters of World War I. In 1917, as part of its war effort under the First Liberty Loan Act, Frost National Bank received and transmitted $474,900 worth of liberty bonds, twice its allotment. As a safe place for security holders to keep those bonds, it inaugurated a Safekeeping Department. And shortly after its modern new bank building opened in 1922, it established a Safety Deposit Department, Trust Department, and Savings Department. Like the nation, and like the Colonel in an earlier era, the bank had survived a war and emerged from it more robust than ever.

In 1926, T. C. Frost Jr. ascended to the Board chairmanship, and his younger brother Joseph Hardin Frost succeeded him as president. Under the aegis of T. C. Frost Jr., assets had soared to $10 million—a far cry from the Colonel's original $3000 investment—and savings deposits had passed the $1 million mark. That year's annual report was guardedly optimistic.

T. C. Frost Jr. would serve as chairman for the next 14 years. Like his father, the Colonel, he was a proud survivor who welcomed outside partners but declined outside help. When he died in 1940, he prided himself on the fact that even on its darkest day, his bank had not had to avail itself of aid from the Federal Deposit Insurance Corporation (FDIC), created seven years earlier to ensure that banks survived the Depression.

As of 1926, however, nobody was depressed. Times were good. Perhaps too good. A nationwide boom in construction and real estate had set off a frenzy of overinvestment in the stock market by individuals and financial institutions alike. As would happen again six decades later, when history repeated itself, everyone thought the good times they enjoyed would last forever. No one could foresee trouble lurking round the corner.

✦ ✦ ✦

It fell upon the broad shoulders of the third Frost Bank president ("Mr. Joe," as Joseph Hardin Frost was and still is affectionately called) to guide the bank through the impending economic catastrophe, the Depression, and later the World War that followed the recovery from the Depression. At some point—the exact moment is uncertain—soon after becoming Board chairman, T. C. Frost Jr. unofficially but effectively passed to his brother Joe the scepter of power as primary bank officer. The younger man would not relinquish that power until his death three decades later.

When he became bank president in 1926, Joseph Hardin Frost was 45 years old, already an industry veteran and fervent preacher of the Colonel's gospel. Today his great-nephew, Senior Board Chairman Tom Frost Jr. (technically T. C. Frost IV but Tom Frost Jr. in this history), says, "Uncle Joe had learned the oral traditions of the bank from his dad and older brother, and he passed them down to us. That ensured philosophical continuity. More than anyone I've known, Uncle Joe embodied the Frost Bank philosophy of integrity and other core values. His principles, which got us through the Depression, were the same ones that got us through our nightmarish ordeal in the Eighties."

Like his two brothers, Mr. Joe was a graduate of Princeton. Like his father, the Colonel, he was a well-read scholar but also a smart businessman who supplemented his erudition with common sense. He was more like the Colonel than any member of his generation, and some of his moves were eerily reminiscent of the man.

Though Mr. Joe is remembered as the most conservative president in the bank's history, certain of his actions seem surprisingly daring today. Just before the Crash of 1929, for example, he engineered a merger with one of the city's most prestigious banks, Lockwood National, on Broadway near Houston Street. Given his ultraconservatism, his insularity, his emphasis on family control and fondness for running a "tight show," that puzzled some observers. It increased the number of "outsiders" on the Board, doubled the number of bank officers, and occurred at a time when mergers were the operative definition of risky business.

But then, had the Colonel himself not bought a bank and taken on outside partners in the 1890s, during a national depression? Mr. Joe may have been motivated by the same goals—to enlist allies, shore up assets, strengthen management, and bolster liquidity for an impending struggle: He may have been furthering what was already a Frost Bank tradition. In any case, the risk paid off. Increasing total deposits to $20 million before the fateful year 1929, it combined one of the community's oldest banks, Lockwood National, with its second largest, Frost National, to create a financial bulwark sturdy enough to withstand the onslaught ahead.

Mr. Joe had foreseen that onslaught. His prescience had warned him that once the real estate and construction booms skidded to a halt, the glut of greedy overinvestment would mean misfortune for banks and a crash for the stock market. History proved him right. As customers frantically withdrew funds to fuel their investments, 5000 banks bit the dust of failure.

But Frost Bank was not one of them. It had not jeopardized its sound assets and liquidity for the sake of growth but reinforced them *while* growing for the sake of solidity. Doing so allowed it to weather the devastating storm of the stock market crash. "Don't talk about how big we are," Mr. Joe had counseled his protégés at the bank. "Talk about how strong we are, how well we take care of customers. And always maintain enough liquid reserves to pay off our depositors if and when they demand it. Liquidity, liquidity, liquidity!" In 1931, with financiers jumping out of windows in Manhattan and hysteria gripping the nation, the advice seemed prophetic. That year, a run on one of San Antonio's largest banks forced it to close. Days later, as Frost Bank depositors queued up to withdraw their funds, Mr. Joe stepped outside to assure them there was cash enough to pay them off and that the bank would remain open for as long as they wished to enter.

The line thinned immediately. Later, the story goes, some customers actually returned to redeposit what they had withdrawn. Frost Bank not only survived the run but became the largest, and reputably stablest, bank in the city. Liquidity, liquidity, liquidity.

The judgment of history, however, is that something even more vital than liquidity enabled the bank to survive the Depression. That something was integrity, a quality which safeguarded depositor trust in this bank after the biggest bank in San Antonio (nameless here) had failed. In the wake of that failure, Frost Bank, which resolutely survived, was perceived as all the more solid and trustworthy. Depositors turned to it.

As stated: In 1914, Mr. Joe's older brother T. C. Frost Jr. had signed for Frost Bank as an incorporator of the Federal Reserve Bank of Dallas. Mr. Joe served from 1925 to 1930 on the board of that bank, and crucially, in 1927—the year after he became Frost Bank president—he was finally able to get a branch of the Federal Reserve established in the Alamo City. He even provided free space for the branch until its building was completed. The branch still operates today. Later, from 1931 to 1936, he served as advisory councilman for the Federal Reserve district that included Texas.

Landing a Federal Reserve branch was undeniably a boon for the San Antonio community. Yet, paradoxically, for all his years of relationship with the "Fed," Mr. Joe's attitude toward it appears to have remained forever ambivalent. Conceivably, though he recognized the need for it, he hoped that his own bank would never have to turn to the Federal Reserve for help. And like his older brother T. C. Jr., he was downright cool toward the FDIC, created during the Depression under Franklin D. Roosevelt, whom he (surprisingly) had supported for president. Though it bolstered depositor confidence in the industry by federally insuring accounts of up to $5000, Mr. Joe contemptuously dismissed the FDIC as a "subsidy for our incompetent competitors."

Chuckles his great-nephew Tom Frost Jr. today, "Uncle Joe was never for the FDIC—even though it helped us indirectly. Uncle Joe just couldn't rid himself of the notion that we weren't *big* enough for the government to step in and save us, and that we'd always have to sink or swim on our own."

Following the post-Depression recovery, Joseph Hardin Frost held the bank together during an even darker crisis: the Second World War. During no national calamity did the bank's beacon shine brighter. With all its bases, San Antonio was the most military American city between New York and Los Angeles at the time. In 1943, the bank opened offices at both Brooks and Stinson Fields, providing full services to the men and women stationed there. It also acted as an agent for the Federal Government in honoring "ration banking" coupons for local merchants desperately needing to redeem them. And it led all San Antonio banks in the sale of War Bonds, War Stamps, and other U. S. Treasury obligations.

By the end of the war in 1945, deposits at the bank had more than doubled in the four years since America's entry. Joseph Hardin Frost had earned the reputation of the shrewdest, soundest money man in Texas. That reputation spread to Mexico, a country greatly loved by him, and by succeeding Frost presidents. Recalls retired Senior Vice-President C. J. Krause, who worked at his side for eight years, "Mr. Joe had a wonderful rapport with Mexico. He spoke fluent Spanish. He was invited often to address the Mexican Bankers Association in Spanish. It was Mr. Joe who had the vision of opening our doors to Mexico by establishing a relationship with its banks." That relationship became a powerful Frost Bank tradition.

In 1948, weary and battle-scarred from a depression and a war, heartsick over the death of his son John Frost II in that war, fearful of another depression like the one after World War I, Mr. Joe left the presidency to become Board chairman. This ascension, however, was not an abdication of hands-on power. Mr. Joe would "run the show" for eight more years, until his death in 1956. When death claimed him at age 76, the bank—indeed the whole community—mourned his passing with shock. The man who could have written banking textbooks on how to survive wars and depressions through ample liquidity, solid assets, sound relationships, and common sense was gone. The man whose First Commandment of "relationship banking" had been to treat every customer, filthy rich or dirt poor, with equal respect was gone. The man for whom being good was an advantage he preferred to being big or famous or lucky was gone.

To those who had known him, or even of him, he had been not just the head of Frost Bank but Frost Bank itself. They could not believe he was gone. Having watched him stand tall, imperturbable, and seemingly indomitable on the battlefield of one national calamity after another, perhaps they had expected Mr. Joe to live forever.

THE THIRD GENERATION: T. C. "Tom" Frost III (1903–1971)

The Alamo City's population doubled during the postwar years of the late Forties and the Fifties that gave birth to the Baby Boomer generation. When its military personnel came marching home to find jobs plentiful and attractive commodities affordable, they were quick to demand suburban homes, automobiles, household appliances, television sets—the appurtenances of the good life. To meet the demands of this generation, Frost Bank would require a new generation of management.

In 1948, when Mr. Joe became Board chairman, that generation stepped forth in the person of his nephew Thomas Claiborne Frost III (Tom Sr. to some), the bank's fourth president. In this history, he is referred to as Tom Frost III, or occasionally as Frost III. Having been born the year the Colonel, his grandfather, died, Tom Frost III had already worked at the bank—in the shadow of his father and uncle—for 24 years. From 1942 to 1947, in the Frost tradition, he had served on the board of the San Antonio branch of the Federal Reserve Bank of Dallas. When he became president, his Uncle Joe conferred even weightier duties and responsibilities on him, though the old man continued to wear the mantle of the bank's principal officer.

The times demanded change. Presiding under the chairman's watchful eye, Tom Frost III was willing to change with them, though not quite as rapidly as they were changing. He rode the horse in the direction the horse was going, as the saying goes. But he rode it with a tight rein. Safeguarding the inviolable Frost legacy—loyalty, integrity, relationship banking, sound assets, and a higher level of liquidity than other banks maintained—was always his top priority. Making money, though important, came second.

The bank's loan policies were traditionally conservative, and those of Tom Frost III were no less so. Even in the boom years of Fifties prosperity, he was painfully cautious about making loans to people new to San Antonio with whom the bank had no relationship. That was, of course, in the Frost tradition. But at times, Tom Frost III's caution struck onlookers as too much of a good thing. If not as circumspect as his mentor, Uncle Joe, he was quite circumspect nevertheless. "I was a little alarmed at Dad's loan policies," confesses his son, Tom Frost Jr. (technically Frost IV), who had become an assistant cashier in 1950. "I was afraid we might lose our market share and another local bank would overtake us. None did, but there was cause for concern."

In other areas, he is quick to add, Tom Frost III was an extraordinarily progressive and innovative president. During his tenure, he moved to decentralize the Frost Bank management: a move some considered radical. He streamlined the bank's accounting system and initiated long-overdue budgeting and planning systems. He established a credit department and (though reluctantly) introduced an all-purpose credit card, the city's first. In short, he gave the bank the organization it needed to develop and grow.

More: He was the Frost chairman who saw the bank install its first computer, ushering in the age of high technology. He recruited bright college graduates from parts of Texas outside the local community and devised a management training program for them. He hired an outside accounting firm for annual audits and accounting guidance, and a major San Antonio law firm to represent the bank. With a visionary's eye to the future, in perhaps his most daring move, he formed the bank's first holding company as soon as the law allowed him to in the early 1970s.

Tom Frost III was also the president who reorganized the bank into separate divisions and implemented a management system whereby genuine authority could be delegated. In the past, committee meetings had been informal gatherings, held around Mr. Joe's desk every morning. Now those meetings, conducted around a conference table, began with formal reports from the heads of each division. The new system entrusted not just more power to the bank's officers but more responsibility as well.

"As for recruiting young officers," Tom Frost Jr. attests today, "those Uncle Joe had brought in during the late Thirties had left to serve in World War II. During the War, we lost a lot of young men to the draft, and they never came back. So our management had gotten old. Dad rejuvenated it."

Tom Frost III's presidency also witnessed the establishment of postage-free bank-by-mail service; an around-the-clock deposit vault; "sidewalk tellers," at the bank's drive-in windows, for automotive depositors; and the construction of a multimillion-dollar motor bank and an accompanying garage that provided parking for 750 automobiles. He may have been a conservative 1950s president, but he was willing to turn as the world turned, and he saw to it that even with his slower pace, the world would not leave his bank behind.

In 1957, Frost Bank deposits passed the $200 million mark. Four years later, another milestone was reached when agreements were finalized with Mexican banks to exchange pesos at an official fixed rate. That marked not just a first for San Antonio banks but a breakthrough in relations between the United States and Mexico. The economy of San

Antonio, the city to which more shoppers and visitors from Mexico flocked than any other, would prosper, and the tradition of Frost Bank's close relationships with Mexican banks would be enriched.

By then the Sixties had arrived. In 1962, when Tom Frost III became Board chairman, his son, referred to as Tom Frost Jr. in this history, was elected bank president. He was only 34. But once again, the top link in the active chain of command would be the chairman, not the president. For nine years, until the elder Frost died in 1971, father and son were to work together in tandem. But who was boss was never in question. Tradition prevailed.

Of their relationship during those nine years, C. J. Krause recalls, "They were a great team. In most banks, a new president had to go before a committee and convince twenty-five people to do something. Tom Jr. only had to convince one: his dad. Things happened fast. The Board always went along with Tom Jr. and his father."

The one thing everybody could predict about the Sixties was that they would be radically different from the Fifties. To remain competitive, banks and other institutions would have to change radically. But how fast was up to them. Working together as one, the young president and the aging Board chairman viewed long-term growth via flexibility and innovative planning as the formula enabling the bank to maintain its market share and position in the community.

In 1963, Frost Bank installed its first computer, an IBM 1401, which it upgraded with an IBM (Model 30) 360 three years later. Skipping the punch-card operations other local banks used for processing and bookkeeping seemed a way to forge ahead into the future with a leg up on major competitors like Alamo National Bank and the National Bank of Commerce. At the time, of course, Frost Bank could hardly conceive of how giant a step it had taken, since computers were ultimately to revolutionize banking even more than other industries.

In 1965, the year Frost Bank opened its new motor bank and parking garage, total assets soared past $300 million. Innovative concepts in marketing, advertising, and correspondent banking were introduced. The rapprochement with Mexican banks and Mexican customers continued to thrive. Before the decade's end, Frost Bank would be prosperous enough to institute retirement, pension, and medical insurance plans for its employees, and to make its stock available to them.

If not historically pivotal, as 1968 would be, 1966 certainly proved a year to remember. It was the year the U. S. Treasury Department requested that Frost Bank launch a new facility at Kelly Air Force Base to service the needs of 30,000 civilian and military personnel. That facility opened the following year as the first permanent branch office in the bank's history.

Nineteen-sixty-six also marked the formation of the Frost Realty Company. Here was one of the boldest and smartest moves taken during the helmsmanship of Tom Frost III—an atypical maneuver, unprecedented in the bank's history but executed (as was the Frost tradition) because industry realities and the age mandated it.

As its name implies, the Frost Realty Company was organized as a separate, or "side," corporation to hold the bank's real estate investments and other nonbanking assets. But it served a more important purpose. Frost Bank needed to establish itself in San Antonio's suburban banking market (as the city stretched itself toward the suburbs) just to remain competitive in the community. But branch banks and bank holding companies were prohibited by law. It had, therefore, become common practice for Texas banks to set up "side corporations," whose stock was held by trustees for the benefit of the stockholders (in direct proportion to each stockholder's interest in the bank), and then direct those corporations to purchase a minority interest of less than 25 percent in suburban banks with friendly ownerships.

This was a circuitous process but within the law. To avail itself of it, Frost Bank created the Frost Realty Company. Acknowledges Tom Frost Jr., "Frost Realty was a giant step in our becoming flexible under my father's leadership. By forming it, he allowed us to branch out into the community and not just do business from our downtown bank. Call it our first real attempt at branch banking."

Another experimental corner turned during the Tom Frost III era was the bank's introduction, two years later, of the city's first all-purpose credit card: a BankAmerica card of sound reputation. This move was the Marketing Department brainchild of the chairman's son-in-law, Donald W. ("Don") Garrett, and it positioned the bank on the cutting edge of the industry. Yet some Frost officers were not keen on it, and one of them was the chairman himself.

Today his son explains, "Dad didn't like the idea of putting those cards in the hands of people we didn't know and couldn't size up face to face. It was contrary to Frost tradition. But I reminded him that it was another way for us to do business outside the downtown office. And that no other Texas banks were doing it. And that we needed to be competitive in the state, not just San Antonio."

"Well," the chairman had groused with reluctance, "I may not like the way the world's turning, but I guess I'll turn with it. Do the card, Tom."

By then, 1967 had become 1968: across the country, a year of rapid and convulsive change in a decade of tumult. For Frost Bank, 1968 was to pose huge risks in community undertakings that would change the face of San Antonio forever. Fittingly, it was also the bank's hundredth birthday. What happened to Frost Bank that year, and over the following 30 years, is recounted in the chapters ahead.

chapter 1

A City Is Reborn: 1968

Frost Bank's tradition of community service had been established by Colonel T. C. Frost before there officially had been a Frost Bank. A hundred years later, in 1968, his great-grandson Tom Frost Jr., 40 years old and bank president for six years, was taking part in decisions that would shape the future of the San Antonio community. As he puts it, "I would propose our taking part in community ventures and Dad would say Yes or No. Those were pretty much our roles."

Often, for the bank's participation in community projects the elder Frost said Yes to, as he generally did, the younger Frost was given the ball to carry. Conceivably, as both architect and engineer, representing his family's fourth generation of bankers, and soon to inherit the mantle of leadership, he felt more responsibility to safeguard the bank's philosophy and tradition than any Frost president before him. He stood as a caretaker between two eras. Though conservative himself, he would become the Frost CEO most daringly dedicated to growth—branching, acquisitions, mergers, and expansions—for growth would become the name of the game in banking, and this industry waited for no man or woman.

In 1968, fueling up for the voyage of its second hundred years, the bank needed to change as never before to remain competitive in the modern age. But if it changed too fast, it could shipwreck its identity as the Frost National Bank, a paragon of caution, conservatism, and common sense. Steering the flagship on a true course would require a steady hand, some perfect sense of balance, and even more of an eye to the future than Frost Jr.'s predecessors had kept, because now the world was changing faster than it had during their turns at the helm.

Of all the traditions Frost Jr. had to uphold, the bank's reputation for core values like honesty and integrity was most sacred to him. At the dawn of a financial epoch historians record as fast-and-loose if not amoral, Frost Jr. might appear to some as *too* principled: a throwback, an atavism. Certain officers retired from the bank feel that were it possible for a banker to be honest to a fault, Tom Frost Jr. was that banker in 1968.

Says one, who has known him since their schoolboy days, "Just look how Tom learned the oral traditions of the bank: sitting at the feet of his dad and his Uncle Joe. Mr. Joe's credo was *'Don't just do the right thing—make sure you do it for the right reason.'* And his dad would ask, *'Tom, how's this gonna sound standin' in front of a judge?'* whenever the subject was something questionable they might have to account for one day. How could the man not be honest to a fault?"

Such talk annoys Frost Jr., who embraces a team concept (the bank is honest, not just the CEO) and deplores the glorification of individuals. He admits, however, that his role models were his father and great-uncle: "Dad was my character mentor. But in the business, Uncle Joe influenced me more. Uncle Joe taught us both everything he'd learned from his own father, the Colonel. My father worshipped Uncle Joe even more than I did."

C. J. Krause, who goes back to the Mr. Joe era, adds, "Tom is a combination of his dad and Mr. Joe. His dad was detail-oriented, whereas

Mr. Joe had the broader vision. Tom is detail-oriented with a broad vision. But his personality is more like Mr. Joe's."

Tom Frost Jr. worked his way up to the presidency. As a teenager in the Forties, he was a mailboy, or runner. After college, which had been interrupted by an Army stint, he became a savings teller. Following a sojourn in Mexico City, studying (at his Uncle Joe's urging) Spanish at the National University of Mexico and working in two Mexico City banks, he returned as an assistant cashier.

Soon he took over the International, or "Foreign," Department. In Mexico, he had realized how vital that country would become to the future of the bank, city, state, and nation. "Mexico is a poor country with a low income," Uncle Joe had told him. "But some day that will change, Tom. Mexico will be a tremendous economic generator." Thus was born the young banker's vision of San Antonio as a national trade and distribution center for goods manufactured south of the border. It would become a tradition for Frost officers to pay constant visits to banking and business friends in Mexico, and to maintain connections with banks in every Mexican state.

Besides running the International Department, Frost Jr., with the consent of his father and his Uncle Joe, set up the bank's first marketing effort (a "calling" or "business development" program to keep in touch with important customers and make new ones); he took a turn at advertising (another activity the bank needed to rediscover); and finally, he attained the pinnacle for any young banker: loan officering. Nevertheless, being elected bank president in 1962 came as a surprise. "I'd been told I would *not* be the one to take over the presidential reins," he discloses, "and that the primary ownership would go through Uncle Joe's branch of the family. But my cousins decided not to be active in the bank. That left just me."

Again, as with the Colonel, destiny seems to have played a hand. Banking had not even been Tom Jr.'s first love; petroleum engineering (his major at The University of Texas prior to military service) had. Yet after the service, transferring to Washington and Lee in Virginia, he dropped petroleum engineering and pursued a B. S. in Commerce. "In the Army," he explains, "I'd realized I wanted to come back to San Antonio to live. But I couldn't as a petroleum engineer. Dad had said there'd be a place for me at the bank if I wanted it. So my decision was based on where, not what. I chose the community over the career."

As stated earlier, Frost Jr. was to go down in the bank's history as the CEO of branch banking, mergers, and acquisitions; as a master of expansion; as the CEO who would grow the bank to proportions undreamed of. But like his predecessors, he was dedicated to growing not just the bank but the community too. In the early Fifties, he had determined that Frost Bank do everything it could, even incur risks and make sacrifices, to nurture and develop San Antonio. It was not a novel idea. Beginning with the Colonel, every Frost Bank president had been so determined, for a bank is only as prosperous as its customers.

Frost Jr.'s vision, however, was not just of a city bigger or wealthier but a city reborn. A great city. With the Sixties, the father-son tandem knew the decade had arrived for San Antonio to make something happen, were it ever to become that great city and not just an overgrown town, sleepy and slow-paced, with Old World charm and grace and a *mañana* attitude. Until then, things had simply happened to San Antonio. First there had been the South Texas cattle industry, for which no one had to plan; then the South Texas oil business. The cattle ranchers and oilmen had come there to live because San Antonio was quaint, easygoing, and lovely, and sure beat living back at the ranch or down in the Oil Patch.

Agribusinessmen had come to set up offices, because South Texas was primarily agricultural and San Antonio its largest town. Next came the military bases, since the location, geography, lay of the land, and weather were perfect for aviation and the stationing of trainees. Many retirees so loved the city, they never left it.

But San Antonio had not made those things happen. Houston

had dug a great ditch—a ship channel—and made itself an international port. Dallas, lacking water access, had made itself a crossroads of trade and distribution, retail, finance, fashion, and transportation. Unpretentious San Antonio had not made itself much of anything—San Antonio simply *was*—and so all it had become was poor (compared to Dallas and Houston) and dependent on the military for economic sustenance.

But how would it survive, wondered the Frosts *père et fils*, were the military to pull out, close its bases? Or pull back, downsize, outsource? The Cold War could not last forever. San Antonio had scant visibility to the world at large other than as a town with a mission: the Alamo. Where would it be without its mission and its military presence? Those were questions politically incorrect to ask in a city more concerned with preserving its past than forging its future.

Frost Bank and other civic leaders knew the city needed jobs, civilian jobs. To create them, it would have to attract new industries: economic generators. And to attract them, it would have to make something big and dramatic happen for itself. Market—the dominant factor in industrial expansion—was expressed as people times money. But a bank could not create market, crusade to make things happen, or tell a community what it should do. A bank could only lend encouragement, advice, organization, conciliation—and money.

In the Fifties, San Antonio made nothing happen for itself. But the Sixties would be a decade of happenings. Soon the community would seek the bank's help in two historic undertakings that would enable it, if successful, to be reborn.

✦ ✦ ✦

The idea of a fair to commemorate the 250th anniversary of San Antonio's founding was first suggested in 1958 by local retailer and Chamber of Commerce member Jerome K. Harris. He proposed a 1968 "Fair of the Americas" to demonstrate the city's "affection for and appreciation of Mexico."

Nothing came of it until 1962, when newly elected U. S. Congressman Henry B. Gonzalez, reviving the idea, expanded the theme to the "Confluence of Civilizations in the Western Hemisphere," including all the Americas: North, South, and Central. The name "HemisFair," though credited to Harris, was coined by the late Keith Elliott, a local columnist who had used it in a headline.

Tom Frost Jr. got wind of the idea at a Rotary Club meeting in 1962, when Rabbi David Jacobson of Temple Beth-El approached him and said, "Tom, New Orleans celebrated its two-hundred-fiftieth birthday with a citywide celebration. Why don't we celebrate ours with a World's Fair?"

A World's Fair! Frost Jr. has admitted that his initial reaction was skeptical. But soon afterward, he got a phone call from local merchant and civic activist Bill Sinkin, later a banker himself. Gonzalez had contacted him, Sinkin reported, with a proposal for an international trade fair to create additional tourism for the city and facilities for permanent government buildings. The Congressman had even promised to secure funding for a Federal Pavilion.

Sinkin invited Frost Jr. to a meeting at the old Plaza (today Granada Homes, Inc.) Hotel at South St. Mary's and Villita Streets. Gonzalez was not there, but a handful of prominent locals were. They voted to commission a feasibility study—financed by the city's 26 banks through the clearing house association the second T. C. Frost, the Colonel's son, had founded in the early 1900s—to determine whether a World's Fair could be held in San Antonio.

As the largest bank, Frost National came up with the largest share of the study's $50,000 cost. When the study (using the 1962 Seattle World's Fair as a paradigm) flashed the green light, Frost Jr. got an okay for the bank's participation—which meant underwriting a hefty chunk of the operating costs—from his father Tom Frost III and the Board. He also agreed to sit on the Fair's executive committee.

Dimly, the banks and other businesses perceived what a World's Fair might mean for the city. It could tap into federal urban renewal funds available for long-overdue clearance and building. It could free up (given the Fair's requirement for automobile access) construction on the stalled but sorely needed North Expressway section of Interstate 37. And it could redevelop the River Walk.

Though it was the city's most picturesque natural wonder, the River Walk had been disgracefully neglected for years. Just two businesses—a Mexican restaurant and the Cullum Dixieland Band's home "The Landing"—operated on the River level. Shops and eateries whose posteriors faced the water kept their back doors locked and bolted. Underlit, underutilized, unattended at night, the River Walk cried out for painting, repair, park benches, sanitary maintenance, increased police protection, a new image. It was a shameful example of the city's Fifties inertia.

In the early Sixties, before talk of a World's Fair, two local businessmen had worked tirelessly to rehabilitate the River Walk and persuade businesses to buy properties on it. They had made calls on existing owners, too, imploring them to open their back doors to the River. One of those men, Jim Hayne, became a Frost Bank Board Member in 1968, the year of the Fair; the other, David Straus, founder of the River Walk Commission, would join the Board in 1985. Straus and Hayne embodied the tradition of Frost Bank Board members who unselfishly gave of themselves to the community.

Once the local banks agreed to underwrite, the Fair hit the ground running. A corporation, San Antonio Fair Inc., was formed, with Sinkin as president and Marshall T. Steves, a director of Alamo National Bank, as chairman of the underwriting committee. In mid-1963, the site was announced as approximately 100 acres just south of Alamo Plaza.

Initially, the banks only underwrote to defray the Fair's front-end expenses, ensure it opened on time, and handle operating costs. Or so they hoped, since the really big bucks would come from the city, state, and federal government: political entities. This fair had friends in high political places. Those friends included (1) a liberal Democrat president, Lyndon B. Johnson, and First Lady—Texans with ties to the Alamo City—who would tout it by inviting 30 foreign ambassadors and their families to a barbecue at the LBJ ranch; (2) a liberal Democrat congressman, Henry B. Gonzalez, who would wangle funding for a $7.5 million Federal Pavilion; (3) a conservative Democrat governor, John B. Connally, who would ramrod state funding for a $12 million Institute of Texan Cultures; and (4) a conservative Republican mayor, Walter McAllister Sr., who would push through bond elections totaling $30 million for the city's one-third share of the urban renewal as well as for a convention center, theater, arena, River channel extension, and $5.5 million Tower of the Americas: the third tallest tower in the world.

As its two-thirds share of the urban renewal cost, Washington granted the city $12.5 million to condemn the site, raze it, and relocate 390 families forced to vacate. Construction would run $71 million. But more than 300 local businesses pitched in with financial support. Thirty-three countries, plus the State of Arkansas, promised to participate.

Despite all that, support for the Fair was not unanimous. There were nasty pockets of opposition in Washington, Austin, even San Antonio. It seems incomprehensible that anyone in Texas, and especially the host city, would oppose the first World's Fair ever held in the South or Southwest. Frost Jr. contends that the problem was not opposition but conflicts of agenda that needed resolving.

Those conflicts of agenda almost closed the Fair before it opened. In Austin, Governor Connally had asked North Texas State Senator Ralph Hall to introduce the HemisFair Bill in the Senate. But Lieutenant Governor Preston Smith, who feuded with Connally and presided over the Senate, refused to recognize Hall. It was not a political impasse whose solution called for a San Antonio banker or a San Antonio brewer. Yet Frost Jr., Harry Jersig (the head of Lone Star Brewery, one of San Antonio's largest employers), and a group of other local businessmen drove to Austin to implore Smith to recognize Hall so the Senate could vote on the bill.

It was a long shot, but somehow it worked. Smith consented, and the bill passed, if narrowly. That broke the Austin deadlock. But the U. S. Senate posed even bigger obstacles. To surmount those, conciliator Tom Frost Jr., like Frank Capra's Mr. Smith, would have to go to Washington.

Again, petty internecine politics were the hurdle. Texas Senator Ralph Yarborough, opposed to anything Governor Connally (the Fair's commissioner general) was for, and not crazy about Mayor McAllister either, was sponsoring bill amendments (1) making it impossible for the Secretary of Transportation to approve expressway projects using lands from public parks, and (2) requiring all historic structures in the Hemis-Fair area to be preserved "to the maximum extent possible" before the U. S. would participate.

Amendment (1) would sabotage the North Expressway, which cut through the city's Brackenridge Park; Amendment (2) would doom urban renewal of the Fair site, where almost any structure could be deemed "historic." Both Frosts at the bank saw Yarborough's opposition as the greatest threat to the Fair; if the U. S. did not participate, why would foreign countries?

There was just one American powerful enough to counteract Yarborough's opposition. When Tom Frost Jr., as part of a posse of San Antonio leaders, asked him for help, that man, President Lyndon B. Johnson, nodded soberly. "I'll talk to ole Raff," he promised. "I want your little fair to happen."

A few days later, having had a change of heart, Yarborough promised not to hinder, if not to help, the HemisFair, and Washington was in.

That left San Antonio. Obstacles there were numerous and exasperating, the hour growing late. Conservationists and architects protested the razing of old buildings and trees. Community leaders decried the forced relocation of 768 people. The Sisters of Incarnate Word College who owned the stretch of Brackenridge Park through which the expressway had to pass refused to sell it.

At the eleventh hour, as things looked bleakest, compromises were reached. The firm of the architect who had howled about bulldozing the environment—O'Neil Ford—ended up designing the Tower of the Americas and extending the River channel into the fairgrounds. City Councilwoman and future mayor Lila Cockrell used her influence to save enough historic structures (some incorporated into the Fair) to satisfy the conservationists. "Mayor Mac" wheedled the Incarnate Word Sisters (who would receive environmental concessions, plus $972,000 in state and city funds) into selling their site after all.

Meanwhile, the Fair was being sold to the Western World. As vice-president of international participation, Frost Jr. sold it in Mexico, Argentina, Chile, Peru, Panama, Colombia, and Venezuela. His staff assistant, Carlos Freymann, sold it in Mexico and Canada. Governor Connally sold it in Mexico and South America, Marshall Steves in Paris and London, Mayor McAllister in Spain.

The mayor also accompanied Bill Sinkin to the five countries of Central America. "We got 'em, too," Sinkin boasts. "But within sixty days, all five presidents except one—Costa Rica's—had been deposed. Little Costa Rica had a grand time at the Fair."

The banks had assumed that a single underwriting would fulfill their commitment. The banks were naive.

Early on, Underwriting Committee Chairman Marshall Steves, who became HemisFair president in 1964, sought $4 million to guarantee a line of credit. When the figure leapt to $6.5 million, Frost Bank participated in asking local businesses to issue guarantees for the bank loans. The first underwriting was guaranteed by a percentage of each admission dollar, secured in a trust from which lenders would be paid later on. Frost also participated with all the other local banks in making loans that would increase to the point of opening the Fair, then decrease with admissions to it.

But when rainy weather and construction delays forced cost overruns, a second underwriting became necessary. Undertaken by National Bank of Commerce President Forrest Smith in March 1968, it recompensed underwriters with HemisFair tickets. Frost Bank Board meeting minutes for that month record a resolution to purchase a sizable number of tickets, many of which would be sold in blocks to megabanks like Chase Manhattan, lending the Fair national exposure. In toto, second-underwriting tickets represented $2 million in new underwriting commitments.

The Fair opened April 6, 1968, right on schedule: a miracle in itself. The 21-story, 496-room Hotel Hilton Palacio del Rio, across Alamo Street from the fairgrounds, had been built in a 202-day round-the-clock blitz by legendary construction contractor H. B. Zachry. Once the base was finished, crews stacked an average of nineteen 35-ton modular rooms per day from the fifth floor up, using a towering crane to slide each into place. The last room went in on December 22, 1967. The hotel opened for business on March 30, 1968, a full week before Opening Day.

But getting the horse out of the gate did not guarantee riding it to the finish line. In less than a month after opening, the Fair was in trouble again—with no money to make payroll. This time, it was Tom Frost III, Tom Jr.'s father, who convened an emergency meeting of the major underwriters at Frost Bank.

The mood was grim. All present agreed that to permit the Fair to close after one month would disgrace the city in the eyes of the world. They approved a third underwriting. They also agreed that the Fair needed new leadership. Unanimously, they voted to grant H. B. Zachry, already honorary chairman and a major underwriter, free rein to take over the project and bring it home. Zachry, inventor of the modular building, was an industrialist of great resourcefulness; a 1970 *San Antonio Light* poll would dub him "the most influential man in San Antonio." Having compiled a track record of bringing in projects against all odds, he had outdone himself with the Hilton Palacio. If Zachry could not save the Fair, who could?

Zachry accepted the committee's offer on one condition. Turning to Tom Frost III, he said, "I'll do this if you'll let your son here raise the money to keep the Fair open."

Frost III glanced at Frost Jr., who nodded; "Done," the older man said.

Working in tandem, Zachry and Frost Jr. estimated that the Fair needed another $3 million to operate for the five months remaining. When the media erroneously reported that Zachry had splurged for the whole sum himself, neither he nor Frost Jr. bothered to correct them. The banker was busy raising that $3 million from anxious, put-upon underwriters. "I explained there would probably be no source of payment," Frost Jr. admits. "This time they were underwriting with a hundred-percent likelihood of being called on it."

The agreement stipulated that no single underwriting would be valid until the entire $3 million had been signed. But that would take time, and a $275,000 payroll had to be met that very day. With no collateral or binding obligation, Frost Bank advanced the Fair the money to make payroll.

By now the bank and the business community were in deeper than either could have imagined at the outset. At some point, the two Frosts taking these plunges must have wondered what the ghosts of Frost Bank—the Colonel, his son T. C. Frost Jr., and the ultraconservative Mr. Joe—thought about banking hundreds of thousands of dollars of the bank's assets on what skeptics had predicted would prove a fiasco. Ostensibly, given their reverence for those ancestors, they decided that, however grudgingly, the ghosts would have approved.

Did Frost Bank get its $275,000 back? It did. The money was effectively funded once the final underwriter had signed, raising the total to $3 million. But there had been no assurance. The risk was tantamount to a fourth underwriting, something no other bank undertook. Frost undertook it because its president and its Board chairman agreed that the damage to the city if the Fair failed would outweigh the damage to the bank if the loan failed.

"We were all anxious," Frost Jr. admits. "After one meeting, an underwriter, Ellis Wilson Sr., sidled up to me and whispered, 'Tom, do you really think we can *make* it?' I said Yes. He asked how."

Frost Jr. then told Wilson a favorite story of his father's about two rabbits chased by a pack of coyotes. When one rabbit asked, "Do you think we can *make* it?" the other rabbit said, "Yes." When the first rabbit asked, "Why?" the second rabbit said, *"Because we have to!"*

HemisFair "made it" because it had to; whatever the expense, the community's banks and businesses could not permit a colossally humiliating failure which would have been theirs too. But the Fair was not a success in numbers or dollars: Its attendance, six million over six months, was far below projections, which had ranged from 7.5 million to 13 million, and it ended up losing between $6 million and $7 million once its cost overruns were paid.

Yet for all that, it was the most successful event in San Antonio history. On the ledgers of the city's future, it would pay for itself a hundredfold. It resuscitated the River Walk, channeling its waters, at a $1.9 million cost, on to the Convention Center (whence they would flow to a million-square-foot shopping and entertainment mall, Rivercenter, 20 years later). Today the River Walk is second only to the Alamo as a visitor attraction.

The Fair's construction also resurrected the downtown area, which today hums with commerce and night life. New hotels—many financed by Frost Bank—sprang up downtown and on the North Side, creating (according to Chamber of Commerce figures) over a thousand new rooms; 2000 motel units were added; hospitality construction enabled the city's convention trade to compete with that of Houston and Dallas.

As an economic generator, HemisFair created 100,000 new jobs in four years. Its Federal Pavilion ultimately became a Federal courts building. Its Institute of Texan Cultures became a permanent tourist museum. Its HemisFair Arena became a home court for the city's first major league sports franchise, the San Antonio Spurs. The Fair gave the community a public relations face-lift. No longer was the city unknown, invisible, to the world outside. Half the people who attended came from states outside Texas, or from foreign countries, and two-thirds came from outside Bexar County; not a few would return later to buy homes and to start up businesses; some had never left.

The National Association of Travel Organizations called HemisFair "the most important travel stimulant in the nation in 1968." San Antonio became the top spot in Texas to visit, surpassing visitor totals of Houston and Dallas combined. More than 57,000 jobs are now supported by the visitor industry, with an economic value to the city of $3 billion; the services sector of the local economy, which includes tourism, is San Antonio's largest employment generator.

Said Frost Jr., "It was the first time in the city's history when every element of the community pulled together to make something happen. Not that we'd always been on opposite sides before. We just hadn't had a compelling event to bring everybody together. I'm proud that all the city's banks got involved. And that we were a major underwriter."

The bank had been not only a major underwriter but the savior of the Fair. It should be remembered, though, that more than community concern or civic pride was at stake. Frost Bank had a huge dollar investment to protect (its 1968 annual report disclosed underwriting payments of $367,000), and a lot of face to save, because Frost Jr. was a HemisFair executive committee member. One should also remember that other businesses took huge risks for the Fair as well.

No one had envisioned everything the Fair ultimately would accomplish for the city. "We knew it would stimulate tourism, give us visibility, and build a convention center," says a Frost Board member. "But none of us foresaw how dramatically it would change the city's face by rebuilding areas in decline, bringing people to town who'd never been here, and attracting economic generators. So we didn't really comprehend what we were doing. But we did it. Mr. Zachry—the real hero of HemisFair, along with Representative Gonzalez—used to say we were too *dumb* to realize we couldn't host a World's Fair here. That enabled us to host one."

✦ ✦ ✦

Frost Bank is proud of its role in another event that happened in 1968, a year Frost Jr. considers the most important in San Antonio history. After HemisFair opened in April of that year, the San Antonio Medical School of The University of Texas admitted its first student the following September.

Historians mark that day as the birth of the community's sprawling 700-acre South Texas Medical Center. Actually, the Center was born five years earlier, in 1963, with the first of its facilities: Southwest Texas Methodist Hospital. As with HemisFair, Frost Bank was a major lender in opening the hospital's doors and then keeping them open.

That story predates the time span of this chapter. But it serves as background to that momentous day in 1968. According to the 1983 book *History of San Antonio Medical Foundation and South Texas Medical Center*, written by Wilbur L. Matthews and reissued in 1997 to commemorate the Foundation's 50th anniversary, the story began two decades earlier, in 1947, when the San Antonio Medical Foundation was created to land a state-supported medical school for the Alamo City.

Previously, San Antonio had been bypassed for Galveston, and then Dallas—a fact that stuck in the craws of Dr. James P. Hollers, the San Antonio dentist who became Foundation chairman in 1956, and Dr. Merton Minter, the San Antonio physician who joined the Foundation in 1962 and succeeded Dr. Hollers as chairman. These men were resolved that San Antonio have a medical school if it took 30 years. It only took 20.

By 1957, the Foundation had spent 10 years seeking a site for the school and Tom Frost Jr. was a Medical Foundation voting trustee. That year also, 23 acres of vacant mesquite pasture in the far-Northwest sector were donated to the Methodist Church for a Southwest Texas Methodist Hospital. The donor, "Five Oaks Inc.," was a consortium of five North Side developers—George W. Delavan, Sr., G. S. McCreless, S. E. McCreless, Edgar Von Scheele, and Carl Gaskin—with concern for the community and visions of developing the area. One founding trustee (as well as treasurer) for the hospital was Tom Frost Jr.

The hospital needed $30 million for construction. Thanks to its influential treasurer, Frost National was the first bank to issue it significant lines of credit, based on collateral from the hospital and guarantees from the trustees. Other banks followed suit, though Frost Bank was the major lender. Unlike the bank's HemisFair loans, these were secured, but they required a leap of faith in a project whose remote location made it initially unattractive and risky.

Once the Five Oaks site was selected and initial capital raised, it took three years to build the hospital. Often Tom Frost Jr. would drive out to the site after Sunday School with his small sons. "We'd look down into this great big hole," he recalls, "which was the only thing out there at the time—and wonder what would ever happen."

What finally happened, in September 1963, was the opening of a five-floor (with two sub-levels) acute care hospital accommodating 175 beds. But that hospital had a medical problem: no doctors. Physicians balked at driving out to the stark boondocks location, and patients were understandably leery of a hospital without them. Within weeks, Southwest Texas Methodist was listed in serious condition. It had run out of money and could not make payroll.

As treasurer, Frost Jr. arranged for a second line of credit, plus working capital, from the bank to cover anticipated losses. But within three months, the working capital was spent. Now the hospital's condition was critical. Frost Jr. then recruited a group of investment bankers who had put together a $1,875,000 bond issue, and Frost Bank made loans to purchasers of those bonds. The hospital was bought enough time to keep from dying in the emergency room. One of those investment bankers who helped save Southwest Texas Methodist Hospital was George Mead, who later managed all Frost Bank's bond accounts and who retired in 1997 as an executive vice-president after 23 years of Frost service.

Southwest Texas Methodist revived when its doctors finally showed up; that encouraged patients to check in. The hospital's life was saved, its immediate future assured. Again, it is important that the bank not be portrayed as a solitary hero. But it did play a significant role. As treasurer and a founding trustee, Frost Jr. had a responsibility to the hospital; and ultimately the bank's loans were paid off. It was simply another instance of this bank's providing transfusions for the lifeblood of a community project.

What had been saved was not just a hospital but the first facility of a great medical center. As Southwest Texas Methodist Hospital was opening its doors, construction crews were breaking ground for a medical school, on a nearby 100-acre tract, that paved the way for a major medical complex.

That school was the spoils of a fierce five-year skirmish—a crossfire with the bank caught in the middle. The controversy, which began late in 1956, weeks before the original Five Oaks donation, centered upon *where* to locate a San Antonio medical school. On one side were prominent downtowners who naturally wanted the school downtown, near the county-supported Robert B. Green Hospital; on the other side were the Foundation trustees, pushing for the Oak Hills site, where Five Oaks Inc. was offering 100 acres gratis.

Advantage lay with the Oak Hills alliance. In 1957, Dr. Hollers was president of both the Chamber of Commerce and the Medical Foundation. And Dr. Minter sat on The University of Texas Board of Regents, which would decide the matter. But the Downtown Group included local potentates Mayor McAllister and his son, Walter Jr.; H. B.

Zachry; and Tom Frost III. These men, along with the powerful Downtown Merchants and Property Owners Association, saw a new medical center as the jolt downtown needed to awaken from its 1950s coma. They had a downtown site blocked out.

Where did Frost Jr. stand? In the middle. He wanted to side with his father, because the downtowns of other cities were dying as new industries flocked to the outer suburbs. Yet he served on the Southwest Texas Methodist Hospital board. What made sense was simply to be on the winning side, since the traditional Frost role was not that of combatant but referee: a conciliator.

In 1959, the battle heated up when the Texas Legislature authorized the regents to "establish a Medical Branch or Department of The University of Texas within the County of Bexar to be known as the South Texas Medical School." The bill was amended by a hostile Dallas State Senator (who thought San Antonio could not comply) with a requirement that a "suitable teaching hospital" be provided "within one mile of the school."

Now the school was a certainty, the battle a war. Clearly, the Downtown Group was doomed to defeat: The Oak Hills donors were offering the regents 100 free acres for the school and 26 more for the teaching hospital. Nevertheless, in deference to his father, Frost Jr. accompanied H. B. Zachry, the perennial miracle worker, on a 1960 trip to Austin, where they met with the regents in a last-ditch effort to plead the Downtowner case.

According to Frost Jr.'s eyewitness account, at one point in the meeting Zachry stood up and smartly slapped two cashier's checks down on the conference table. One check was signed by the National Bank of Commerce, the other by Frost National Bank, and each was for half a million dollars. "Here we have it," the industrialist announced. "The city pledges this money to purchasing downtown land in the vicinity of its county hospital, the Robert B. Green."

It was a dramatic gesture—but the regents did not keep the checks.

When Frost Jr. returned to San Antonio, he described the incident to the Board chairman. "Dad," he predicted, "those regents aren't ever going to build a medical school downtown. They want a medical center with unlimited room to expand in a pristine rural environment. What they don't want is to get involved in downtown urban renewal hassles."

The elder Frost nodded glumly. "Well," he said, "maybe we should support them. We have to do what's best for the community. We may not like the way the world's turning, but we have to turn with it."

In 1961, Bexar County voters approved a $6.5 million bond issue for the construction of a medical school and (the Dallas State Senator's) teaching hospital, with $1.5 million to go for rehabilitation of the Robert B. Green. Two months later, the regents chose the Oak Hills site. They also strongly urged groups in San Antonio "to acquire at least another 150 acres adjacent to the site so that the Medical Center will have available 350 acres for long-term expansion."

It was not an urging but a directive. The regents wanted another 150 acres as the site of a major health science center and related facilities. They wanted the medical complex of which Drs. Minter and Hollers had dreamed for 20 years. Where San Antonio got the money for that acreage, those facilities, was San Antonio's problem.

In 1962, Dr. Hollers appointed a 22-member land acquisition committee to raise money for the purchase of 400 additional acres. The chairman, Sid Katz, Jewish yet prominent on the board of the Methodist Hospital, had been a key player in securing the original 200-acre land donation from the Oak Hills alliance. Colorful, engaging, possessed of boundless energy, Sid Katz had made a fortune in the shoe game, then gone into the oil business, but his passion was community development. He wanted a medical center for San Antonio as much as Drs. Minter and Hollers did, and he was just as willing to fight for one.

From 1962 to 1966, Katz bargained for almost 600 acres of land adjoining the medical school. The total cost would exceed $2 million. The first contribution came out of his own pocket. He set about raising the rest from local businesses, beginning with a downtown bank of note. Tom Frost Jr., whose hands were full with the hat he was passing for Southwest Texas Methodist Hospital, admits to some hesitation. "Sid was asking for such a huge amount of money—for such a vast amount of land—that it seemed excessive," he explains. "When he came to the bank, I was hoping Dad would say Yes but afraid he'd say No. They met privately."

Once Katz had left, Frost III came out of his office. "Look, Tom," he said to his son. "I know you're a trustee of that foundation. And I think it's a wonderful project. And I admire the fact that this fellow Katz is putting his own money into it, not just other people's.

"We're gonna help him," the Board chairman added—and the young banker breathed relief. With the bank's aid, Katz attained his $2 million.

But it was not enough. The Foundation and taxpayers were shocked and dismayed to learn that even after successfully voting bonds and securing matching (federal) Hill-Burton funds, the operation of the teaching hospital and health science center would require a greater amount every year than their original cost. Dr. Hollers lamented, "There was a time when I was naive in thinking that after a legislative act or a bond issue had been approved for a project, half the battle was won. Now I know, after several years of experience, that it is just the beginning." Alarmingly, in this instance, there was no money to fund the rest of the battle.

Belated calculations had established that the maximum levy allowed by Texas law on Bexar County property—$0.75 per $100 of assessed value—would not yield enough funds to pay the bond service and meet the estimated $16 million in yearly operating expenses. To fulfill such obligations, county hospital taxes would have to be doubled. That unhappy knowledge sent Tom Frost Jr. on one of the grimmest errands of his career. Against all odds, armed with little more than a prayer, he accompanied a contingent of influential taxpayers who asked County Judge Blair "Bruzzie" Reeves to cast a swing vote doubling hospital taxes in the district.

"I can't," the judge groaned. "It would be political suicide. Raising taxes will defeat me next time around."

"Please, Bruzzie," the contingent urged. "The community needs this."

"I can see that…" groused the judge, weakening. "Will you at least support me for reelection?"

Judge Reeves cast the swing vote for an amendment to the state statutes. It provided for assessment of property in a hospital district at a greater percentage of cash market value than was used to assess property for general state and county purposes. Tax revenue to operate the two facilities was thereby assured. In the next election, with the support of a loyal contingent of influential taxpayers, the judge was reelected. And two years later, in September 1968, the medical school admitted its first student. The teaching hospital admitted its first patient four months later.

✦ ✦ ✦

Today the University of Texas Health Science Center at San Antonio is one of six facilities in the country federally approved to administer experimental cancer drugs never before given human beings. The Medical Center is the largest medical complex in the state and the third largest income/employment generator—after the service industry (which includes tourism) and the military—in the city. And Frost Bank continues to support the medical community with its involvement in programs like Project Quest, established to recruit, train, and qualify unskilled workers for the sort of jobs needed at the Medical Center.

"I guess we made the right decision about the location," jokes Frost Jr. today. "But there were no winners or losers in that controversy. The winner was the community. I'm glad our bank was able to help make it happen. Still, other banks helped too. We were a supporting player. The heroes were people like Sid Katz, Dr. Hollers, and Dr. Minter.

"As with HemisFair," he adds, "none of us dreamed how much the Medical Center would mean for San Antonio. In the final analysis, the community deserves the credit, because it made something big happen for itself."

✦ ✦ ✦

As always, the bank's traditional willingness to change with the times was evinced by its determination to equip itself with state-of-the-art technology. By 1968, the brave new world of high tech had arrived in San Antonio, and this bank had taken steps to welcome it. Here are three examples:

(1) The core (memory) of its IBM 360 computer was doubled to process electronic demands more efficiently. Frost National became one of the state's first banks to establish an "on-line" data transmission network for its dozens of correspondent banks;

(2) a second IBM 360 was ordered, to lighten the full-time workload of the first as well as that of the (older) IBM 1401; and

(3) the bank's data processing center, a division of Frost Realty Company, proudly celebrated its second birthday in December. In 1966, the bank had purchased Data Processing Center, Inc. from its owner, Robert ("Bob") Guthrie, after leasing it for years to process for other banks and businesses.

The world of loan policy had changed too. During the first nine years of the Sixties, thanks to HemisFair and the Medical Center, Frost Bank's had liberalized. Total loan volume at year-end 1968 was $130 million, up from $54 million in the grey-flannel days of 1959.

Nineteen-sixty-eight also saw the bank raise its loan limit for one borrower to $1.5 million, a sum calculated via the formula *Loan limit equals capital plus surplus divided by 10*. For the year, the bank's permanent surplus increased by $2 million. In November, for the 18th consecutive year dating back to the Mr. Joe era, $500,000 was added to that surplus. The single largest transfer of funds in Frost history, it brought the surplus-plus-capital total to $15 million. Hence the $1.5 million loan limit. This is not a piece of bank trivia. Rather, it illustrates the Frost tradition of constantly augmenting its reserves, its way of saving up for a rainy day that, sooner or later, was sure to come.

The Sixties were a decade of dramatic economic gain for American women. In 1968, the bank created a Women's Special Services Department to cater to female customers and recognize women's importance in the economic community. A year earlier, in 1967, Lois Scott—at one time Tom Frost III's secretary—had been promoted to assistant vice-president: the first woman to attain that rank. She was also the first female bank employee empowered to make loans.

Since the early Fifties, a dozen years before the voice of feminist Betty Friedan was heard, the bank had not only boasted one of the city's largest female work forces but aggressively promoted women into positions of authority. In 1950, Gertrude Eberhardt became its first female assistant trust officer; in 1951, Edna I. Woodruff became its first assistant cashier. These may not seem like such momentous events, but they did make bank history, and demonstrate the Frost tradition of treating employees fairly without being forced to. Today, at this writing in 1998, in an industry still regarded as a good ol' boy fraternity, 57 percent of Frost Bank officers and 69 percent of Frost Bank employees are female.

Nineteen-sixty-eight had been a glorious centennial for Frost Bank and an equally glorious 250th birthday for San Antonio. The bank emerged from that year with renewed vigor, greater confidence, a younger image, a willingness to take risks. San Antonio emerged from it as a city reborn, a good town ready to become great. Both had won crucial battles. Yet neither had violated its traditions, compromised its identity, or deviated from the spirit of its past.

The bank's 1968 annual report closed with this sentence, which understated the case: "If Colonel Frost could see the Frost Bank today, he would be pleased at its growth and progress that are the direct outgrowth of his early labors."

Colonel T. C. Frost early in 1895, at the age of 61

Opposite page, top to bottom: 1887 check drawn on T. C. Frost private bank signed by T. C. Frost; 1898 interim check drawn on T. C. Frost & Co. bank just before national charter granted in 1899; Frost Bank tellers' windows as they appeared in 1892. This page, top to bottom: T. C. Frost Jr., the Colonel's eldest son; $5 currency note issued by Frost National Bank in 1919 signed by T. C. Frost Jr.; $5 currency note issued by Lockwood National Bank of San Antonio in 1907; $10 currency note issued by United States National Bank of Galveston (USNB) in 1923 signed by E. H. Kempner.

49

SIGNERS OF RESERVE
BANK CERTIFICATES AT LUNCHEON
ADOLPHUS HOTEL MAY 19, 1914

Opposite page, top to bottom: May 1914 Adolphus Hotel luncheon for signers incorporating new Federal Reserve Bank in Dallas (T. C. Frost Jr. sits at extreme lower left). Main Plaza, with San Fernando Cathedral and old Frost National Bank building, in 1914. This page, clockwise from upper left: Joseph Hardin ("Mr. Joe") Frost: a legend in his own time. Builder Quincy Lee, the 1930s Frost Bank recruit who became a Board member and Audit Committee chairman. Bandstands, San Fernando Cathedral, and new Frost National Bank building, the city's tallest, circa 1927.

51

Opposite page, top to bottom: Frost Bank Board Chairman Tom Frost III, left, and son Tom Frost Jr., inspecting the bank's 1963 annual report. Mock-up display of bank's first computer, an IBM 1401, in 1963. This page, top to bottom: First two autos in line for 1965 opening of new Frost motor bank and parking garage. Original entrance to HemisFair '68.

Top left: Industrialist H. B. Zachry, a HemisFair hero in 1968. Top right: South Texas Medical Center champion and fund-raiser Sid Katz. Center: Entrance to San Antonio's trailblazing UT Health Science Center. Bottom: Historic 1969 Frost Bank Letter to Stockholders announcing the acquisition of D. Ansley Company, Inc., Mortgage Bankers, as a wholly owned subsidiary.

FROST NATIONAL BANK

T. C. Frost, Jr.
PRESIDENT

POST OFFICE DRAWER 1600
MAIN AT COMMERCE STREET
SAN ANTONIO, TEXAS 78206

June 19, 1969

To Our Stockholders:

Through a wholly owned subsidiary formed for this purpose, the Frost Bank has a contract to purchase 100% of the outstanding capital stock of D. Ansley Company, Inc., a mortgage banking firm of many years service to San Antonio and South Texas.

The transaction has been approved by the Comptroller of the Currency and is to be completed by July 15, 1969.

D. Ansley Company, Inc. will continue to operate as a separate corporation directed by its present management from its offices in the Majestic Building.

Very truly yours,

President

TCFJr:rgc

54

Clockwise from upper left: Donald W. Garrett, Frost Bank president from 1971 until his untimely death in 1973. New Frost Bank Tower as it appeared in 1973. Parkdale State Bank, Corpus Christi, was in 1974 the first Frost bank outside San Antonio.

Top left: Retired Frost Bank president and Board chairman Corky Sledge. Top right: Retired Cullen/Frost holding company president (and still a Board member) Robert S. McClane. Center: Tom Frost Jr., right, with Mexico Secretary of Commerce Fernando Solana, left, and Mexican Trade Fair Director General Adrian LaJous, center, at Plaza Club ceremony, September 1977. Bottom: The late Angelo Drossos, who enlisted Frost Bank's crucial support in bringing the Spurs to San Antonio.

chapter 2

Between Two Eras: 1969

Nineteen-sixty-nine, though not so eventful as the previous year, was not without Frost Bank and San Antonio history-making. As the Sixties' last hurrah, bridging the gap between two eras, it could be called a year of greatness in transition.

In January, as scheduled, the teaching hospital at the Medical Center admitted its first patient and the second IBM 360 computer was installed at the bank. Those two events, though unrelated, got the year off to a roaring start. With new storage devices, the two 360s held capability of direct access to four times the information previously possible; and with its first teaching-hospital patient, the Medical Center was no longer a dream but a *fait accompli*.

The bank's involvement with the Medical Center, however, was not a "thing accomplished" but an open-ended process. The dean of the Medical School, Dr. F. Carter Pannill, had announced that education and training were needed in treating patients as whole beings, with minds and souls, and not just as physical bodies. To that purpose, Episcopal Bishop Everett H. Jones, the Frost family's minister, was urging the Medical Foundation to create an Ecumenical Center.

A small tract of land in the complex had been proposed for one. But as usual, there was no money to buy it. Frost Bank learned that the proposed site was owned by one of its neediest customers, Southwest Texas Methodist Hospital, which was still strapped for money. Unhesitating, Frost Jr. suggested that the Myra Stafford Pryor Trust, which was administered by the bank, consider a $25,000 grant to the proposed Ecumenical Center that would enable it to purchase the land from the financially ailing hospital.

It seemed a way of paying, not robbing, Peter to pay Paul; yet it got the job done. The Myra Stafford Pryor Trust said Yes; the hospital was $25,000 richer; the new Ecumenical Center for Religion and Health opened its doors in 1973. It later moved to a larger facility in the complex, but continued to serve the same purposes as when founded.

Nineteen-sixty-nine also heard a trumpet call heralding the bank's expanding scope and flexibility. On July 14, Frost Bank acquired 40-year-old D. Ansley Company Inc., Mortgage Brokers, as a wholly owned subsidiary. The move signaled a strategic foray into the terrain of long-term commercial mortgage lending.

That was an unwalked path, though the bank had dabbled in traditional short-term interim financing for customers *with whom it had a relationship* involved in long-term commercial projects. Now the bank was flexing its muscles. D. Ansley was a major player in the commercial mortgage game of San Antonio and South Texas, and acquiring it secured strong ties to more than a dozen of the nation's largest, most powerful insurance companies.

Typically, insurance companies were the "institutional investors" in large commercial projects for which Frost Bank, through D. Ansley, could make major loans. But those loans, made only against prior commitments, and sold to the investors, did not impact liquidity. D. Ansley never had to borrow to carry inventory, since no inventory was held for its account. The beauty of this mortgage firm was that its service volume could show a profit even during years when construction slowed to a crawl. The strategy gave the bank a "conservative hedge" against hard times ahead. Frost Bank was to own and operate the mortgage company for 13 years, during which D. Ansley made loans on some of the biggest new office buildings, hotels, and shopping centers in San Antonio.

Retired loan officer and Banking Group head R. E. ("Buster") Fawcett Jr. recalls, "At the time, it didn't fit our lending philosophy to tie up large sums of money in long-term commercial real estate projects. In 1969, that wasn't the proper role for a bank to play. But D. Ansley was project-*oriented*. It dealt with giant insurance companies like Connecticut General that were impersonal by nature. D. Ansley didn't have to look at people first, like we did. It was a perfect fit for us."

The bank was growing by leaps and bounds; by 1969, it had 88 officers and 524 staff members to coordinate. Some of its newer officers recruited by Tom Frost III's Sixties youth movement yearned for greater decision-making authority. That year, the chairman acknowledged a need for management restructuring to keep the bank on its fast-growth track without derailment. He implemented a three-pronged management reorganization:

(1) The Marketing and Credit Groups would be merged into a "Banking Group" to better coordinate sales and credit functions;

(2) the Investment Group would be assigned more and larger responsibilities in the use and allocation of the bank's financial resources; and

(3) the Administration and Trust Groups would be subdivided to empower more officers to make key decisions quickly.

The shakeup was not just a reshuffling of names and titles. Like many of Frost III's innovations, it was surprisingly modern, moving toward a decentralized power structure to expedite decision making. It created tightly coordinated divisional management. Never again would the bank operate as a vertical monolith, run by a single person from the top. It was the way the world of not just banking but American industry itself was changing. The bank changed with it. One of its traditions since the Colonel's days was to adapt to the times.

That November, as part of the change, three executive vice-presidents became group heads: Clyde Crews—Investments; Donald W. Garrett—Banking; and C. Linden ("Corky") Sledge—Administration. Beverly Rust was named chairman of the Trust Committee. All were Texans, since the Frost policy was to grow management from within rather than without, hiring (and then promoting) people who knew and understood the communities the bank served because they had been born, raised, and educated in them. To this day, the tradition of Frost management with firm roots in the Texas community endures; because of that tradition, and not some provincial prejudice, Harvard MBAs and such are rarer than unicorns at Frost Bank. In any case, the three new executive vice-presidents and the new Trust Committee chairman were colorful homegrown products, deserving of thumbnail résumés:

• Sledge, a Beaumont native and silver-haired John Connally look-alike destined to become president and Board chairman, was Tom Frost III's first recruit (out of The University of Texas) for his trainee program in 1956. "Corky" was a "people" person who himself excelled at recruiting and training;

• Garrett, handsome and fun-loving but a hard-driving workaholic, had been a marketing and advertising dynamo at San Antonio's Lone Star Brewery before marrying Ilse Frost, Tom III's daughter, and taking over the marketing department his brother-in-law, Frost Jr., had set up in the Fifties;

• Rust, an attorney out of The University of Texas Law School, and a 27-year veteran at Frost Bank, was an easygoing sort, better at lawyering than managing, but a tough hombre if provoked, since his unfortunate first name demanded it;

• Crews, a World War II Navy veteran and SMU alumnus who

had joined the bank (as assistant cashier) in 1957 and set up its credit department, was another workaholic, determined to learn everything he did not know about banking even if it meant working around the clock.

They formed a solid management cadre. When the tumultuous decade of change drew to a close, the bank was poised for greatness as the largest financial institution in the city and the ninth largest in the state. During the Sixties, its loan volume had tripled. Total dividends for 1969 had doubled to $1.50 per share on the 264,000 shares outstanding. Book value had soared to $81.87 per share. Even the bank credit card, a question mark one year earlier, had taken off: By year-end 1969, the number of cardholders had reached the anticipated projection for 1973. Revenue earnings outstanding for the card exceeded those anticipated for 1978.

If the Fifties had been an overly conservative decade in which the mature median age of the bank's senior officers had kept it from enjoying as much growth as its competitors, the Sixties had been youth-oriented: The bank's fresh-blooded marketing and development efforts enabled it to reorganize for growth and keep pace with its competitors. But while the Sixties radicalized America's culture, they did not radicalize this bank's. Somehow, the entrenched Frost philosophy and values remained intact. The decade was an era for Frost Bank to move forward, as did San Antonio, one step at a time, but with bolder and bigger strides than it had traditionally taken. To paraphrase Tom Frost III, "As the community's world turned, so turned the world of the bank." The two were inseparable.

chapter 3

Harder Times Ahead: 1970–1976

One tradition of Frost Bank, dating back to its earliest years, was to be "proactive" rather than "reactive"—to anticipate problems and confront them directly, before they appeared, like uninvited guests, rudely demanding attention at its doorstep.

With the Seventies, as the city burgeoned into the suburbs, the bank had to expand soon or lose market share. Both Tom Frosts working there knew it. This bank did not lust for bigness per se ("Don't talk about how big we are," Mr. Joe had warned in 1933, when it became the biggest bank in town, "talk about how strong we are and how well we take care of customers"), but it needed to branch out to continue serving customers who had moved to the suburbs and did not relish driving all the way downtown to bank. It needed to turn as the world was turning, and the world of urban America was turning away from the inner city, toward the suburban fringes.

Yes, Frost Bank needed to branch out. But it could not. State law forbade branch banking. And federal law prohibited banks from becoming holding companies that owned banks. So through its Frost Realty Company, Frost Bank continued to maintain ownership of slightly less than 25 percent (as allowed by law) in three banks remote from downtown: Texas State on the East Side, Harlandale State on the South Side, and Citizens National in the Northwest sector. For all practical purposes, Frost controlled two of those banks and exercised potential control of the third. Additional ownership by Frost directors gave it virtual control of all but Texas State, where a decisive chunk of ownership lay in the hands of merchant-turned-banker Bill Sinkin, a loyal Frost friend and ally. If push came to shove, Frost *could* control all three banks.

That was "branch banking" after a fashion—another illustration of the famous Frost flexibility or adaptability—but not the real thing. Texas banks, including Frost Bank, were manacled. Yet change was in the wind. In 1970, with amendments to the Bank Holding Company Act of 1956, Congress would finally allow banks to become bank holding companies. Given its stock interest in other banks, Frost Realty Company soon found itself registering with the Federal Reserve Board as a bank holding company.

That was history-making indeed, for now it appeared that the manacles had been removed. Recalls one high-ranking Frost officer, "Texas banks jumped in as soon as the law changed. A Houston bank bought a Tyler bank. When the State Banking Commission screamed branch banking, the Houston bank threatened to take it to court. The Banking Commission backed down, and the state's first bank holding company saw the light of day uncontested. Now it was incumbent on us to get started on our holding company."

The start was attempted with a Frost filing to bring into its holding company the three "neighborhood" banks over which it exercised nominal minority ownership but effective control. "Since we can be a bank holding company," reasoned Frost executives, "why not own the whole bank instead of twenty-four-point-nine percent of it?"

It was a rational argument. But the U. S. Justice Department, a watchdog of bank mergers and acquisitions, was not a rational animal. It ruled against the filing. "You're too dominant in the San Antonio market already," it scolded the Frost representatives. "Any bigger share owned by you would impede competition." Tossing a sop, the Justice Department allowed Frost Realty to bring in one of the three banks, Citizens National, since Frost Bank had been involved in its 1961 start-up.

Angrily disappointed, Tom Frost Jr. flew to Washington D. C. to convince federal antitrust authorities that Justice was wrong. He argued that the San Antonio market was segmented over too vast an area for the three neighborhood banks to compete with any other bank, Frost Bank included.

"No," they insisted. "Justice is correct. You can't buy an existing bank in San Antonio. Buy one someplace else. Or start up a San Antonio bank *de novo*."

Inwardly, the banker fumed. "Since we're that dominant back home," he asked with wry sarcasm, "may we use your ruling to advertise the fact?"

"No," replied the authorities humorlessly.

But they had suggested a genuine detour around the roadblock: *de novo*, or brand-new, banks. Detours, when other paths failed, were consistent with the Frost tradition of flexibility. In December 1972, Frost Realty Company agreed to divest itself of interests in the Texas State and Harlandale Banks for prompt approval to found "a broader-based holding company." Those divested interests would be sold at a profit used to establish banks *de novo*.

The die was cast. In May 1973, Frost Realty Company was reorganized as FrostBank Corporation, a "broader-based" bank holding company, with Corky Sledge as president. Now the initial but thwarted quest for a holding company undertaken during the watch of the late Tom Frost III would be realized by his son, Tom Frost Jr.

The new holding company's immediate move in 1973 was to

acquire Citizens National Bank by merger, as had been approved by vote at a special stockholder Board meeting in August 1972. Its second major move in 1973 was to create, as the antitrust authorities had suggested, two *de novo* banks: Colonial National, at Wurzbach and Interstate Highway 10, and People's National (later Liberty Frost), at Blanco Road and West Avenue. Both banks would open in 1974; when they did, FrostBank Corporation would be a four-bank holding company.

With four banks in the works and things on a roll, why not go for five? In 1973, since the Washington regulators had suggested buying a bank in some other town, the holding company set sights on Corpus Christi.

Moving into another city was a big step and a big risk, not unlike a person's leaving home for the first time. Corpus Christi was the city for it, though. Corpus Christi was South Texas—native turf; Frost Bank had numerous correspondent banks and a community image in the Coastal Bend area. In 1970, when the tropical Hurricane Celia had struck, Frost Correspondent Banking Department members rushed supplies, food, water, and personal necessities to Corpus Christi, and the citizenry had not forgotten it.

On May 4, 1974, FrostBank Corporation acquired 16-year-old Parkdale State Bank, with $27.4 million in deposits. The significance of that event can scarcely be overemphasized. It set a precedent for mergers and acquisitions in the future. Parkdale State was not only Corpus Christi's fourth largest financial institution but squarely in the path of the city's rapid southward growth. History was made and policy set. From that day forward, the company would merge with or acquire only banks having solid assets and strategic locations.

"Liquidity, liquidity, liquidity" went the bank's leitmotiv, and now a second line was added: "Location, location, location." Frost was still a community bank, but now that community truly was South Texas, not just Bexar County and its environs.

Back in Bexar County, the bank had outgrown its 50-year-old home. Minutes for a specially called Board meeting in October 1970 indicate unanimous approval for a new bank building. Ground was broken in May 1971. A 20-story 400,000-square-foot Frost Bank Tower with a 750-car parking garage, one block north of the old facility, was to face on Houston Street, between Main and Flores. The Tower would become the biggest building downtown, as had the old Frost Bank edifice constructed in 1922.

Not that size mattered. On the subject of size, witnesses recall conversations in the planning stage between the Board chairman and project architects. "How tall do you want your building?" they had asked Tom Frost III.

"What's the most *efficient* height?" he replied. "That's how tall I want it!" The response became a piece of company lore. Clever though it was, it said more than it seemed to; by efficient, Frost III meant focusing on customer needs first, with an eye to the future, rather than on the bank's "wants." With Zen-like economy, the reply encapsulated Frost relationship banking and its priorities.

Daily, crowds of gaping gawkers watched the mighty Tower rise. A 70,000-pound climbing crane with a 120-foot boom was raised from floor to floor hydraulically, hoisting 3500 pounds of steel at a time. The crane was then dismantled on the roof and lowered to the street in sections. The building was topped out on September 5, 1972, with red-white-and-blue steel beams, Old Glory, and a Christmas tree.

Bringing home the project on time, within budget, had been the impossible task of Kenedy, Texas, native Robert S. McClane, a future holding company president. In 1962, McClane had been hired out of Trinity University for the Frost training program. The physical and operational side of the business was his forte. The Tower was his first major project. A hands-on perfectionist, a taskmaster who demanded things be done his way, McClane was involved with conceptualizing and designing the Tower from Day One. "Organizing was our major challenge," he recalls. "We'd asked key officers at the bank to plan for their specific needs. But it was hard to get people who think present tense to envision what size the bank would grow into, or how technology would affect the way we'd work, or what new things we'd need to house our areas."

Day and night, McClane relentlessly rode herd on the mammoth project. By September 1973, just 28 months after groundbreaking, the Tower was open for business and bustling with activity. Almost 70,000 people visited it during a first month that saw a windfall of new deposits.

But the man who would most have loved to see it never lived to; in a sense, the Tower was a monument to him. After 47 years of service, Tom Frost III had died in January 1971. Fittingly, his last breath was drawn at Southwest Texas Methodist Hospital, whose life his bank had helped to save. Two months later, in March, J. H. ("Joe") Frost Jr.—Mr. Joe's son, the senior Board chairman since 1962—died also.

As per Frost tradition, the succession was unruffled and orderly. Tom Frost Jr. was elected Board chairman, and his brother-in-law, Don Garrett, replaced him as bank president. "Now I was on the spot," Frost Jr. recalled years later, hinting that it may have been lonely at the top without a mentor, a father, calling the shots. Actually, he was more than qualified to be chairman, having now worked at the bank during four decades and served almost 10 years as its president; additionally, since 1967, he had been a director of the local branch of the Federal Reserve Bank, in a term that would not expire until 1972.

Two years after his father's, untimely death struck again. In February 1973, seven months before the Tower opened, Don Garrett dropped dead of a heart attack at a bankers meeting in New York City. He was only 44. It was another grievous loss: Garrett had been a fear-less, hard-driving leader who could analyze any problem and resolutely pursue a path to its solution. It was Garrett who had set up every detail of the new marketing department Tom Frost Jr. initiated in the Fifties, and who had engineered the bank's advertising renaissance as well.

Corky Sledge, elected at the February 1973 Board meeting, replaced

Garrett as bank president while remaining president of FrostBank Corporation. Reportedly, a few days after Garrett's funeral, Frost Jr. had told Sledge, "You're it, Corky. You're the guy right next to me now." One can imagine what emotions Sledge felt at that moment.

✦ ✦ ✦

Nineteen-seventy-three was the year of the infamous "Arab Oil Embargo." By October, America was importing one-third of its oil. That month, OPEC (Organization of Petroleum Exporting Countries) clamped an embargo on the United States as punishment for its support of Israel. Americans were pained to discover that the halcyon days of cheap, abundant oil were over as they endured a grim winter of lowered thermostats and speedometers, lines of cars at service stations, and the beginnings of a recession.

But Texans were not just Americans but Super-Americans. Since the embargo meant increased dependence on domestic oil, it spelled economic bonanzas for Texas, the foremost oil-producing state. That was good news for Frost Bank. As Texas fared, so fared its banks, and the state, with its "black gold," would hardly be vulnerable to a recession triggered by an energy shortage. One top-echelon Frost Bank officer reminisces, "What was happening at the bank overshadowed anything happening nationally. This was a time of tremendous activity and excitement for us. We were building a new home, a new holding company, and helping the city get a major-league sports franchise. We were even getting into indirect automobile financing. Texas banking was progressing at an exhilarating pace. Texas was a world unto itself—and we were right in the middle of what was happening there."

The mention of indirect automobile financing is important. This service, a contractual assignment taken from car dealerships at their discretion, allows a bank to approve a customer's auto-finance application and finance his purchase without meeting the customer. That the finance contract goes (today by Fax) from car dealer to bank makes the service "indirect." In most cases, the buyer gets a better interest rate, and the bank gets business it would not have otherwise. For Frost Bank today, this service begun in the early Seventies means $300 million in loan volume outstanding.

As the bank officer said, a whole lot was happening. In 1973, D. Ansley broke records as dollar amounts of mortgage loans serviced reached an all-time high and loan closings exceeded those of any previous year. In 1974, the newly chartered *de novo* banks, People's National and Colonial National, opened in April and June respectively. Corpus Christi's Parkdale State Bank joined the Frost fleet in May. But harder times lay ahead. The euphoria dampened late in 1974, when the corrosive recession finally seeped into Texas and the bank encountered its first loan problems since the Depression.

Bad loans are the bane of a good bank's existence. The mid-Seventies were the heyday of the REIT (Real Estate Investment Trust), an aggressive and speculative real estate instrument allowed by income tax codes to sidestep corporate taxes. REITs borrowed money by the bushel to buy and develop Seventies real estate. Up to 1974, they had been so successful that bank holding companies were using them as ancillary vehicles.

But that year, the vehicles developed engine trouble. "We got involved as a lender with one," says a Frost loan executive, "that was owned by three major southeastern banks. When the REIT failed, we had to take over the loan. And it was a big one. Other real estate loans at the time had deteriorated too. But it was good for us to confront the problem and work our way through it. It prepared us for what happened in the Eighties."

Nineteen-seventy-four was also the year Frost's ALCO Committee was created to balance and control interest rate risk. Says retired Chief Investment Officer George Mead, "When I joined the bank in 1974, Tom Jr. had just formed the ALCO. I was an original member of that

70

committee. Later, bank examiners insisted that banks work harder at managing their interest rate risk. But we had a leg up—we'd done it before they made us. And we weren't in the kind of trouble other banks were."

The national recession deepened in 1975. Climbing interest rates throttled economic activity; loan demand slipped badly; as the slump hit its nadir, Frost Bank was busy building up its stockpile, annually increased by tradition, of capital reserves. As a result of provisions for loan losses, net income that year dropped to $1.84 per Frost share: a 37 percent decrease from 1974's $2.92. But the bank was wisely treading the water of traditional conservative policy. It was better to be safe than sorry.

"I remember that time," says Tom Frost V, Tom Jr.'s eldest son (at 47) and today a senior vice-president. "It was worse than people recall. It scared me away from having anything to do with loans or credit. I saw the toll it was taking on people I knew and loved." Tom Frost V (born Tom Frost III but referred to in this history as Tom Frost V) joined the bank in 1975. The following year, during the nation's bicentennial, as the bank got back on track after its minor derailment, it felt confident enough to set up a cash management service, with Tom Frost V as head. The service was a noncredit operation that essentially said to astonished commercial depositors, "Hey, you've got too much money sitting with us. Why not let us help you invest it faster and keep less of it here?" A smash hit, the service immediately generated steady noninterest income for the bank in the form of fees. Everybody profited.

Explains Frost V, whose avocation is songwriting and whose 1970s Citizens Band handle was The Singing Banker, "Starting up the cash management service gave me a chance to work at the bank in a non-lending capacity. It was either that or be a musician, and I didn't like the hours there. I jumped at the chance. I've never regretted it."

The nation's bicentennial was significant for the bank's International Department too, as 1976 saw a devaluation of the Mexican peso. Steadfastly, while other banks refused, Frost Bank continued to exchange pesos. For years, Tom Frost Jr. had been making speeches in Spanish and drawing thunderous applause with the line "There's no reason to import goods from foreign countries like Detroit and Pennsylvania when we have Nuevo Leon right next to us." Now was the time to prove he meant it.

During the early Seventies—a politically troubled era for its friend south of the border—the bank doubled its loan amount to Mexico. But even then, its Mexican deposits were 10 times the doubled amount. This was the decade in which Luis Echeverria Alvarez was president of Mexico and trade fairs were the mode of developing international commerce. Frost Jr. played a key role in convening groups from both sides of the border for those fairs. Along with Mayor Charles Becker, he succeeded in bringing innumerable Mexican businesses to San Antonio— and into Frost Bank. Indeed, the Frost correspondent bank business in Mexico and its long-established reputation for understanding the customs of Mexican businesspeople were enhanced through those trade fairs.

"Quite frankly," Frost Jr. said at the time, "San Antonio is like a Mexican city in many ways. Businesspeople from Mexico feel comfortable here." Twenty years later, in the NAFTA and NADBank Nineties, Mexico would remember the community that had been its staunchest Texas ally.

For the most part, the bank emerged from its toughest ordeal since the Depression with flying colors. Counting its suburban affiliates, its 1976 local market share was 26.5 percent of all Bexar County deposits. Its Corpus Christi bank closed out the year with a deposits increase of 11 percent over 1975. The Frost tradition of calmly weathering storms while promptly confronting problems had prevailed.

Yet the bank remained unsatisfied, restless. It yearned to enlarge its community presence in the state and expand into bigger markets that might earn it national recognition. It began to cast eyes on the Bayou City: mighty, booming Houston.

Meanwhile, Frost's newly venturesome home base, San Antonio, continued to take risks in the form of civic gambles for which the bank lent support. It is common knowledge that Frost was the major bank lender for the hefty cost of landing the city a professional basketball team. The San Antonio Spurs would earn the community more prestige and recognition in the nation's eye than a dozen Chambers of Commerce could have.

The Spurs were the dream of the late Angelo Drossos, a stockbroker and former used-car salesman with extraordinary negotiating skills and tenacity. In the early Seventies, Drossos approached Tom Frost Jr. and asked if he thought the city would support pro basketball.

"Well, Angelo," replied the banker, "we'll never know if we don't try." With that reply, San Antonio sports history was made.

"I just got a feeler by phone," Drossos disclosed. "The Chaparrals are for sale or rent. They're Dallas's ABA basketball team, and they're looking for a place to move."

It was a long shot, Frost Jr. knew. The American Basketball Association was an upstart league, looked down upon by the older NBA and in danger of folding. The Chaparrals were pathetic losers who had compiled a 25-54 record the previous year. Texas was football, not basketball, country. And if Big D could not support pro basketball, how could San Antonio? But the banker also knew what it could mean for the city if the gamble paid off. He was willing to buck the odds. He committed the bank to a million dollar loan, half of it to lease the Chaparrals for two years (with an option to buy), the other half for working capital.

Before Drossos went to work rounding up local investors to guarantee the loan, Frost Jr. advised him to collar enough of them so that no guarantor would suffer unduly if called on his commitment. Drossos talked 34 pillars of the business community—entrepreneur B. J. "Red" McCombs and Marshall Steves (of HemisFair renown) were among the first—into plunges that ranged from $20,000 to $100,000.

Frost Jr. recalls one day when, lunching at the old St. Anthony

Club, where many a deal was done by handshake, he watched Drossos hop from table to table with a notepad. "He'd give folks his pitch, then write their names down with the amount they were in for," the banker says. "Later, we'd meet at the bank and he'd show me the list. I noticed on the notepad a man's name at the top that was scratched out. Then I'd see it somewhere else: scratched out again. I asked what it meant."

"Oh, him?" Drossos chuckled. "He's a friend who keeps coming by when I'm not looking and crossing his name off. But I always put it back on." The friend finally gave up—and became a major investor.

Drossos quickly raised $800,000. He then went after budding young hoop stars who might transform the loser into a winner. Before he died, he described to the author of this history how, one evening in 1973, he made a call to Frost Bank from New York, where he had been drinking and dealing with Earl Foreman, owner of the ABA Virginia Squires.

"I delivered the best pitch of my career," Drossos boasted. "Twenty minutes later, in the New York Federal Reserve, $300,000 had been put through to Foreman's account by Frost Bank. I called our coach, Tom Nissalke, and said, 'Guess what? I just bought you a center.'"

That center was Swen Nater, the Squires' flagship player. The next month, Drossos made another call to Frost Bank. This time, he talked Board member/loan officer Clyde Crews into committing the bank to forking out another $225,000. "He said he had to buy one of Foreman's classy young guards," Crews recalls. "He wouldn't take No for an answer, so I finally said Yes." Saying No would have been a mistake. The classy young guard would ultimately win four NBA scoring titles and become the greatest shooter in the game. His name was George Gervin: the "Iceman."

The Chaparrals-turned-Spurs quickly became a moneymaking ABA title contender. In 1976, when the ABA disbanded, they were one of four franchises absorbed by the NBA. But the entry fee was steep: $6 million.

Again, Drossos prevailed upon Frost Bank. But this time, Frost Jr. insisted that he get other local banks involved also—not just to spread the risk but to give the Spurs broader business support and enhance their position in the community. The city's two biggest other banks—Alamo National and the National Bank of Commerce—came aboard, as did the Broadway Bank. Soon, the $6 million loan was paid off as the Spurs started winning divisional titles and becoming a top NBA draw.

Frost Jr. never became a Spurs owner, though he would have liked to. He declined the opportunity on ethical grounds: conflict of interest. But Frost Bank remains the Spurs' bank to this day. "My family is the Spurs' biggest fan," Frost Jr. claims. "We still sit in the same season-ticket seats we purchased twenty-five years ago."

Frost Bank continued to be a loyal financial supporter of the Medical Center as well. Back in 1971, Don Garrett, the bank's new president, had agreed to raise a million dollars (matched by federal Hill-Burton funds) for the complex's new Cancer Therapy and Research Center (CTRC). When Garrett died in 1973, Medical Foundation Trustee Dr. J. M. Smith told Frost Jr., "Tom, now you have to raise that million."

The banker accepted the challenge. He spearheaded a drive to raise the money. As usual, estimates had run too low; the CTRC opened in 1974 at costs of over $2.5 million, and additions would ultimately hike them to $6 million. But it was money well spent: Today this outpatient treatment facility saves human lives and performs vital research on the ever-elusive cure for cancer.

Another loyal supporter of the Medical Center was the Good Government League, or GGL—a group of powerful, conservative, mostly Anglo businessmen who had imposed on San Antonio an uneasy but effective political consensus since 1955. GGL candidates invariably won. They were committed to act in the interest of the whole city, which had an "at large" system of electing the mayor and council. Like a board of directors, they kept out of the day-to-day business of running San Antonio while setting policy for it.

The GGL drew its last breath in 1976. Some felt it had died three years earlier, when one of its own, Handy Andy supermarket chain magnate Charles Becker, broke rank and ran for mayor as an independent. With Becker's victory, a feud broke out between the old, established business community downtown and the "Young Turks" developing the north suburbs.

In 1974, when Becker revealed that the city had been paying the Greater San Antonio Chamber of Commerce a cool million a year to attract new industry to San Antonio, the young Turks revolted and started up their own Chamber of Commerce, on the North Side. That year, to heal the schism, General Robert F. McDermott, then president of not just USAA (United Services Automobile Association) but also the Greater Chamber, founded the Economic Development Foundation (EDF). It transferred the civic task of attracting new businesses from the public sector to the private. Sold on the idea, 34 local businesses coughed up an entry fee of $10,000 apiece to finance the selling of San Antonio.

Frost Bank was among them—but just one of the 34, no more active than the others. Nevertheless, joining the EDF would buy it trouble. In 1975, the bank found itself in the middle of a political maelstrom. Two years earlier, a grass-roots pressure group called COPS (Communities Organized for Public Service) had surfaced in the Alamo City. COPS was a hodgepodge of political have-nots, chiefly low- to-middle-income Mexican Americans, who used the Saul Alinsky technique of rude and loud confrontation to pressure the business community into supporting sorely needed capital improvements on the West Side.

Why COPS zeroed in on Frost Bank as a tactical target is uncertain; prominence and visibility were surely factors. Also, the bank was an EDF member—and COPS was convinced the EDF was not just selling but selling out San Antonio to relocating firms as a "cheap-labor" town, like some Third World metropolis ripe for exploitation. On an afternoon in 1975, 200 COPS members swarmed into the bank and tied up tellers for hours by forcing them to change pennies for dollars.

That month, COPS troops also invaded a prominent old downtown department store, Joske's of Texas, and spent hours trying on expensive clothes but buying none. But such tactics could not compare to those of its invasion of the Frost National Bank. Tom Frost Jr. did not know that even as he listened patiently to its demands in his office upstairs, COPS was exchanging pennies for dollars in the lobby downstairs. "They slapped us while we were turning the other cheek," he recalls today with a touch of rue.

Though smarting from the slap, the chairman heeded the advice of a veteran employee he often looked up to, C. J. Krause. "Tom," said Krause, "those are good people. They're fighting for their neighborhoods. We should try to understand where they're coming from." In the effort to do so, Frost Jr. read the Saul Alinsky tactical manual, *Rules for Radicals*, and then circulated copies of it to bewildered EDF members. "I told them they had to read it to understand why COPS did what they did," he explains. "I told them COPS had a goal we could live with."

Once again in its traditional role as community conciliator, Frost Bank took the lead within the EDF to try to work with COPS. It was like pulling teeth, and equally as painful. But the persistence paid off. EDF members never became Saul Alinsky disciples, nor did COPS ever join the EDF (or its spin-off, United San Antonio), but COPS and the business community did learn to work together. The Metro Alliance and Project Quest, vehicles for community job training and placement, were two results of such cooperation. School bond issues and vital drainage projects would demonstrate it as well. The joint effort continues today. "We have a happy relationship with COPS," Frost Bank says—and means it.

✦ ✦ ✦

Groups like COPS, or the ideas they espoused, spelled doom for the GGL. In 1976, the national bicentennial, the Justice Department gave San Antonio an ultimatum: Adopt a single-member districting system or explain why not in court. The City Council battled over the ultimatum; by one vote, it changed the city charter to allow for 10 council districts, each electing its own member, with only the mayor elected at large. GGL loyalists reacted with cries of outrage. Ironically, the deciding vote had been cast by the last GGL candidate ever elected; in the Eighties, that council member would go on to become mayor and the single most dynamic figure in the community. His name was Henry Cisneros.

The districting change sent a message: The good old days of GGL unanimity were gone forever; partisan community activism and inter-district squabbling, with the mayor as referee, would replace them. But Tom Frost Jr. accepted the change as not just inevitable but healthy. "It was the way the world was turning," he explains. "It brought people face to face with participatory democracy. Not only were you represented in government, but now you were part of it. Never again would decisions about community growth and development be made by a select group at the top." Those words were reminiscent of the managerial power-structure reorganization his father had pioneered at the bank during his final years.

The mid-Seventies saw the tradition of Frost community involvement not just continuing but gathering steam. In 1975—the year the bank's president, Corky Sledge, was also president of the Greater San Antonio Chamber of Commerce—Robert S. McClane began a three-year term as the chair of an exciting new civic organization called Leadership San Antonio. It was partly due to McClane's recommendation that the Chamber had adopted Leadership San Antonio, which was based on a similar program launched in Atlanta in the Sixties.

Essentially, Leadership San Antonio brought together local leaders of diverse ages, background, and ethnicity from a cross-section of professions—business, the military, nonprofit organizations, the public sector—for the purpose of learning about key parts of the community outside their own spheres. "Its greatest contribution," says McClane, "was a larger understanding of the whole community than had ever existed before. That enabled city leaders to pool their resources, get things done that needed doing, and build for San Antonio's future." The program, some 40 members strong and co-sponsored by the Hispanic Chamber of Commerce, remains active today.

✦ ✦ ✦

Long before the EDF made headlines, Frost Bank had worked for community economic development as a private company. Says a long-time bank employee, "Whenever we would hear about firms moving to San Antonio, we'd do everything we could to assist them and their families to get here."

The support this bank lent major companies relocating, and others starting up from scratch, varied greatly. In some cases, it took the form of loans that closed the deal to form a company; in others, loans to construct new quarters or to expand existing ones; in others still, encouragement, moral support, sharing its knowledge of the community, extending a friendly hand, even sitting on a board. In the Sixties, for example, J. H. ("Joe") Frost Jr., Mr. Joe's son, had been taken with an upstart computer firm later known as Datapoint and destined to become the city's largest manufacturer and civilian employer. Tom Frost Jr. himself has sat on the boards of Dr. Robert V. West's Tesoro Petroleum Corp. (in 1968 the city's first publicly traded company); Sam Barshop's La Quinta Motor Inns, Inc.; and Southwestern Bell Telephone Company, later Southwestern Bell Corp., or SBC.

According to the *San Antonio Express-News,* San Antonio's personal income index almost doubled (the growth was 95.6 percent) between 1971 and 1976. That leap reflected the migration of new companies to the city. Confidentiality forbids disclosing the names of Frost Bank customers, though the number was substantial.

During the first wave of belated economic growth that began in the Sixties and extended into the early Eighties, the city was blessed with economic generators like Tesoro Petroleum Corp., Fox Photo Products Inc., and La Quinta Motor Inns, Inc.; Valero Energy Corp., Diamond Shamrock, and SAS Shoemakers; Harris Corp., Kinetic Concepts Inc., and Levi Strauss & Company; Advanced Micro Devices, Mark Industries, Sprague Electric Company, Cafeterias, Inc. (Luby's Cafeterias), and Nationwide–WAUSAU. Those are just a handful; there are many others, and the mid-Eighties, with its high technology, would bring a second wave.

Not all the new companies succeeded or lasted. But most did. Many companies came as the result of stubborn effort by public organizations like the Chambers, the EDF, United San Antonio, and Target '90, working in concert with private businesses. And no private business extended itself more in such effort than Frost National Bank. Lending a helping hand to newcomers was nothing new for it but furthered a tradition begun a century earlier, when Colonel T. C. Frost lent every ounce of support he could muster to settlers seeking new lives and a better deal as they passed through Main Plaza.

Conventions are the economic lifeblood of big cities. In the early Seventies, San Antonio found itself in desperate need of major conventions for its economic growth. The problem was the lack not of a first-class convention center—HemisFair had built one—but enough first-class hotel rooms to accommodate conventioneers. Frost Bank recognized the problem; by itself, however, there was nothing it could do.

After the flurry of construction triggered by HemisFair, the city's downtown resurgence had lapsed into a lull, as if developers, builders, and entrepreneurs had imposed a hiatus. Nor was there the hoped-for lessening of economic dependence on the five military bases. "And why should there have been?" the *San Antonio Express-News* would ask in its decade-end recap. "The Vietnam War was still in full swing, and San Antonio's economy was bubbling with lots of Air Force recruits and gobs of government spending."

But America's part in the Vietnam War was over by 1973. And downtown, particularly around the HemisFair site, still cried out for redevelopment. HemisFair, according to Chamber of Commerce statistics, had created over 3000 new hotel and motel rooms, a third of them downtown, bringing the citywide total to 7000. But six years later, in 1974, the city sounded an emergency alarm for a thousand more rooms.

The alarm was finally heeded during the bicentennial year, 1976, which saw a redoubled effort for downtown redevelopment. Downtown hotels, vertical parking garages, apartment complexes (some on the River), and new office buildings began to rise. The city got its thousand hotel rooms. In the general area of HemisFair, a $10 million Plaza Nacional/Four Seasons would open in 1977 and a $20 million Marriott Riverwalk in 1979. The 291-room La Mansion del Norte (on Loop 410) would also open in 1979, and the Riverwalk's $50 million Hyatt Regency San Antonio, proposed in 1975, would host its first guest in 1981. The conventions came. The city was on the move again. Over the five years from 1976 through 1980, it grew by 11 percent, almost triple the national average for cities.

What was Frost Bank doing all this time? In addition to enjoying its substantial San Antonio banking business, it was also financing downtown projects, particularly hotels. Other banks were doing their fair share; and with some hotels, Frost was not involved. Still, during this era, hotels new to San Antonio had no better banking friend. The citizens reciprocated by putting one dollar of every four they deposited into the Frost National Bank.

81

chapter 4

Cullen/Frost Bankers, Inc.: 1977

7-7-77. Four lucky sevens. Like some heraldic bearing, they are emblazoned on the bank's history. July 7, 1977, was the day FrostBank Corporation merged with a three-year-old Houston holding company, Cullen Bankers, Inc., to form Cullen/Frost Bankers, Inc.

The merger created the eighth largest holding company in the state, with over a billion dollars in deposits. For Texas it was the banking event of the year. And for Frost Bank, it also meant a listing on its first major league stock exchange—the Nasdaq, or National Association of Securities Dealers Automated Quotations—with CFBI as its ticker symbol.

FrostBank Corporation shareholders would own 69.8 percent of the holding company's outstanding stock, and have two more banks making money for them: (1) eight-year-old Cullen Center Bank and Trust in downtown Houston—the ninth largest bank in Harris County, with deposits of $216 million, and (2) Dallas's Citizens National Bank, 10th largest in Dallas County but the biggest downtown bank unaffiliated with a larger holding company. The Cullen Center Bank, incidentally, had broken records on the day it opened in 1969 by recording a whopping $28.8 million in deposits.

It was the Frost interests who had approached the Cullens, not vice-versa. The "feeler" had occurred somewhere between two national recessions; yet that was not inconsistent with Frost tradition. Colonel T. C. Frost had taken on partners during a national depression in the 1890s, and Mr. Joe had merged with Lockwood National just before the Crash of 1929.

But *why* merge? For the same reasons the Colonel and Mr. Joe had: to bolster assets, enhance liquidity, and ally the bank with winners who shared its philosophy and values. Another reason was to put its name on the big map. The Frost name was dominant in San Antonio and South Texas, but the outside financial world did not know much about those places. What it knew of Texas was Houston and Dallas: boomtowns with big bucks. The bank, therefore, would go into Houston and Dallas. Additionally, it would profit not just San Antonio but the whole state to present a broader financial visage to the world than just two cities. Frost would now operate in four markets comprising half the population of Texas. The financial world would *have* to sit up and take notice.

FrostBank Corporation's invitation to the Cullens had gone like this: "You're the biggest entity in Houston or Dallas not a major holding company. We're the biggest entity in San Antonio not a major holding company. We know we can't get there without you. We think you can't get there without us. Let's join together." It was a persuasive pitch, yet the Cullen response had been guarded. "We'll get back to you," it went. "We're sort of used to being in control of ourselves."

The Cullens were not being coy. As the more conservative of the two companies, they were nothing if not circumspect. Says 68-year-old Roy H. Cullen, grandson of the patriarch Hugh Roy Cullen and a principal negotiator, "Usually, people take a while before they embark on such a move. We consulted our stockholders. And they decided maybe the time was right for a merger."

Those stockholders, whom some Houstonites called "The Family," were not just Cullens but also families into which the Cullen sisters had married: the Arnolds, the Robertsons, and the Marshalls. Other shareholders included three more Cullen Center Bank and Trust founders: Quintana Petroleum financial advisor W. Oscar Neuhaus; his cousin, the prominent Rio Grande Valley businessman Vernon ("Doc") Neuhaus; and Mrs. Vivian L. Smith, the widow of Houston oil legend R. E. ("Bob") Smith. Cullen Bank President Robert G. Greer and Board Chairman Dee S. Osborne were shareholders also. None of these denizens were exactly lacking for references, but the Cullens emanated a very special family aura. "Those Cullens are just like sterling," Doc Neuhaus once remarked to Tom Frost Jr. "You can count on their character as being pure."

As promised, the Cullens got back to the Frost team. Judiciously, the latter suggested a partnership in which the Cullen name—the Houston/Dallas imprint—would appear first. Earlier, however, Frost asked this question: "What is your primary aim in forming a holding company with us?"

"To build value for future generations," the Cullens replied.

It was the reply the Frost team had hoped for. The question was not rhetorical. Frost suspected how similar the Cullen philosophy was to its own but wanted to hear it firsthand, as the answer to a direct question. Emphasizing relationships. Putting customers above projects, with depositors first, honesty foremost. Developing the community. Building value for shareholders. These were time-honored traditions of both families.

The family histories revealed uncanny parallels. Like the Frost family, the Cullen family boasted legendary figures in two centuries. Ezekiel Wimberly Cullen had left his Georgia plantation in 1835 to practice law in the East Texas town of San Augustine. That year, seeking adventure and a cause, and inspired by the Texas revolt against Mexico, he rode with Ben Milam's raiders into San Antonio and helped drive out the Mexican army. Later, in the House of Representatives of the Third Congress of the Texas Republic (1838-39), while serving as chairman of the Education Committee, he sponsored the Cullen Act, which created land endowments for public schools and laid the cornerstone for public education in Texas.

His grandson, Hugh Roy Cullen, was a 20th Century patriarch. Hugh Roy's meager public education took place in San Antonio. At 16, he worked as a cotton broker, but soon went into real estate. After entering the Houston oil business in 1918, he drilled enough gushers to be dubbed "King of the Wildcatters"; in the Twenties and Thirties, his fabled oil discoveries in Southeast Texas included the O'Connor Field, the most famous of wildcatter oil fields.

Hugh Roy Cullen was to the state's independent oil business what Colonel T. C. Frost was to its independent banking. Like the Colonel's, his word was his bond. He succeeded in the hazardous and complex business of drilling for oil partly because his earlier careers as cotton broker and real estate dealer had established his reputation for honesty and earned the trust of his peers. Business acquaintances correctly rated his credit as far sounder than that of Texas banks at the time.

Like the Colonel and Mr. Joe (the other Frost legend), Hugh Roy Cullen believed that responsibility for the growth and development of a community lay with the private sector. By 1955, he had donated 95 percent of his immense wealth to religious, educational, medical, and cultural causes. The University of Houston, the Houston Symphony, and the city's world-famous medical facilities are three such recipients. Philanthropy became a family tradition; today the Cullen Foundation Hugh Roy established in 1947 dispenses annual grants averaging $11 million to medicine, education, and the arts.

The new holding company listed as CFBI wasted no time in nurturing the tradition of community activism common to both families. The financing of a costly hotel renovation in downtown Houston and that of a NASA facility in Clear Lake for a prominent space company were soon proof of its commitment to that tradition. The Bayou City was the richer for what had happened on 7-7-77.

With the catastrophic year 1983 six years away, it appeared that the merger was a marriage made in heaven. Nobody walked, or was let go; Frost and Cullen officers blended like university alumni at a football game. Cullen officers would work in Frost banks; Frost officers would work in Cullen banks; ultimately, officers from both camps would work in financial centers like Galveston's United States National Bank (USNB), which the company had not yet acquired. Today's USNB president, in fact—F. A. ("Andy") Odom—had been with the Cullen bank for four years prior to the 7-7-77 merger, and would be dispatched to the Galveston bank in 1982. Recently retired Cullen/Frost Vice-Chairman J. Gordon Muir Jr. began as a credit officer at the Houston Cullen bank, worked at an Austin bank in which the Cullens had an interest, presided over Dallas's Citizens National Bank, and finally returned to Houston as chairman of the Cullen bank, where he had begun. The company's officers are nothing if not mobile, flexible, adaptable; one could cite other, equally circuitous voyages.

During the first quarter following the Cullen merger, Frost shareholder earnings increased by 36 percent and the newly assembled holding company reported assets approaching $1.5 billion. In 1978, net profits would increase by 21.8 percent over those of 1977. The huge, prosperous Houston market and community were in the Frost fold—and 1983 was still a long way off. Roy H. Cullen announced, "We're very happy we've merged, because it's turned out great for everyone. We had only been in banking eight years. We needed to get with people like the Frosts, who'd been bankers a long time. Their steady philosophy and traditions were invaluable to us. And we had the same viewpoints about treating employees and developing the community."

✦ ✦ ✦

Not long after HemisFair, Frost Bank loan officer and Board member Clyde Crews, a Lutheran, had persuaded the Frost Executive Committee to approve emergency loans for the South Texas Medical Center's proposed Lutheran General Hospital project. Because another local bank had withdrawn at the last minute, the project had asked Crews to submit its loan application to his bank. The Frost committee agreed to lend $750,000, as requested.

But then nothing happened. As with Southwest Texas Methodist Hospital, the problem was that doctors hid from the remote location. "Clyde," Tom Frost III finally asked in 1970, "aren't you a Lutheran?" When Crews nodded, the chairman said, "I want you to get on that hospital board and see what's going on."

Crews recounts, "I went to Vernon Moore, the pastor of St. John's Lutheran Church, and asked, 'How do I get on the Lutheran General board?' He asked Why, and I replied, 'Because I think I'd like to serve on it.'"

"You're on it," the pastor had proclaimed.

Soon doctors appeared, if initially from Mexico and Cuba. Several years and several cost overruns later, the 161-bed hospital opened as St. Luke's Lutheran on June 6, 1977. The ultimate cost was $10 million, of which Frost Bank financed approximately $1.2 million, or $450,000 more than originally requested. It was the first private hospital in the Medical Center directly affiliated with the University of Texas Health Science Center at San Antonio. Today, reflecting medical ecumenicism, it is called St. Luke's Baptist, and Clyde Crews, 10 years retired from Frost Bank, is still serving on the hospital board, which is now part of the Baptist Hospital System.

The story affords one more example of the bank's resuscitation of a Medical Center project. It also illustrates the tradition of Frost Bank officers volunteering for health industry board posts. Tom Frost Jr., a trustee of both the Medical Foundation and Southwest Texas Methodist Hospital, serves on the Health Science Center's development board. His youngest son, Patrick, now Frost Bank president, currently sits on the

Finance & Audit Committee of the Santa Rosa Health Care Corporation, and on the board of the Cancer Therapy and Research Center (CTRC) at the Medical Center. Tom Frost III, Frost Jr.'s father, served as first chairman of the Baptist Hospital development board and was succeeded in the post by another Frost Board member, Jim Hayne; Executive Vice-President Kenneth A. Trapp, who as of 1998 heads up the Frost Retail Division, has also served on that board.

More: Frost Trust officer Frank Pancoast helped put together the merger that resulted in the multi-hospital Baptist Health System. The current Cullen/Frost Board chairman and CEO, Dick Evans, chaired the Medical Foundation board from 1992 to 1994. This list, which is virtually endless, evidences the bank's unflagging commitment to health care. Its equally strong commitment to education is demonstrated in a forthcoming chapter.

In 1979, both commitments were affirmed by the official registering and chartering of the Charitable Foundation of Frost National Bank—a nonprofit instrument through which Frost member banks could make charitable gifts to the communities they served. All funding would come from the banks themselves. Health care, education, human services, and the United Way were—and are—prime recipients of Frost Charitable Foundation gifts. At year-end 1998, almost 20 years after the chartering, total Foundation assets would stand at slightly less than $2.4 million.

Nineteen-seventy-seven was the year Congress passed the Community Reinvestment Act, or CRA, which resulted in a vital new department for the bank. An industry milestone, the CRA was a Carter Administration attempt to ensure that financial institutions serve the whole community, including low-income areas, and not just affluent sectors. It did not specifically target racial or ethnic groups, though they may have been part of its concern.

In the case of Frost Bank, the CRA directed it to do what it had been doing all along—but more efficiently, with minutely detailed record-keeping. In immediate compliance, the bank's CRA Department was established in 1977. In the words of Bernard Gonzales, who has headed up that department during most of the Nineties, "We had *always* been actively involved with the whole community, not just the affluent communities or suburbs, and *always* taken care of the inner city from our downtown location. But now we would keep more detailed statistics of our lending involvement in low-income areas, to low-income and minority applicants, and to small businesses, which generate job growth."

The facts bear Gonzales out. Existing records indicate that back in the early Seventies, prior to the CRA, Frost Bank's denial rate for loans to low-income and minority applicants consistently ran at least 15 percent lower than those of the local MSA (Metropolitan Statistical Area, which encompasses Bexar, Wilson, Comal, and Guadalupe Counties), and that its bookings for such loans regularly ran at least 15 percent higher. Even in 1990, 13 years after CRA passage, as Texas banks were still recovering from the setbacks of the Eighties, Frost Bank booked 63 percent of all loan applications it received from low-income applicants. The local market booked just 32 percent. That margin is almost unbelievable.

Throughout the Nineties, Frost has continued to outperform the local market in every CRA category. In 1994, for example, it booked 58 percent of its applications for home improvement loans from low-income applicants while the market was booking only 34 percent—and its denial percentage was 18 points lower than the market's. That same year, its booking percentage for home purchase loans to such applicants ran 19 percent higher than the market's and its denial percentage 26 percent lower. That year also, its bookings of loans for home purchases to census tract-designated "minority" populations bettered the market's by 15 percent, while its denial rate was 10 percent lower.

Today the bank keeps its detailed records of CRA compliance

with a plethora of sophisticated software introduced in the Nineties, notably the CRA "WHIZ." This gadget tells it whatever it needs to know within seconds about any block in the city: demographics, number of small businesses, family census figures, what loans have been made to what families at what addresses. The aptly named WHIZ owes its existence to the CRA Act, as does the Frost Progress Loan Program, established in 1991: an outreach effort to provide flexible loan underwriting for trustworthy citizens lacking established credit. Like the CRA Department, the Frost Progress Loan Program is one more example of the bank's reinvesting in the community, thereby sustaining the dynamic of bank-community synergy that has existed since 1868.

Beverly Rust retired as chairman of the Trust Committee in 1977. During his eight-year tenure, the 52-year-old Frost Bank Trust Department had become the largest in South Texas. Today it is regarded by some as a precious jewel in the Cullen/Frost crown. The corporation's 1998 trust assets, including those of its Galveston and (new) Dallas/Fort Worth offices, run close to $12 billion.

A trust is a legal fiduciary arrangement in which one person, business, or institution holds title to property for the benefit of another. Bank trusts may simply hold assets to provide tax advantage and legal protection, or manage them to provide active investment and financial planning. Banks manage trusts and estates in order to act as a full-service provider for the banking needs of families and businesses. Trusts are also a source of substantial fee income for banks.

In 1919, trust powers had been issued Frost Bank by the Federal Reserve Board; in 1925, the bank officially established a department to handle its expanding volume of trust business. Forty-five years later, at year-end 1970, that department's assets stood at $225 million; at year-end 1976, at $395 million; and in 1979, at $564.154 million. By then the department was administering farm and ranch holdings, oil and gas assets, city real estate, even securities portfolios.

By the late Seventies, trust fees had become a godsend to big banks because it was getting harder and harder to make money off *loans*; increasingly, interest made from loans did not greatly exceed interest paid out from deposits. So Frost Bank found itself paying more attention to noninterest-related activities. Another blessing conveyed by the historic 7-7-77 merger was that it deposited fresh trust bounty into the holding company's coffers.

By year-end 1976, the one-year-old trust department of the company's Dallas bank, Citizens National, already boasted assets of over $7 million. But $7 million was peanuts compared to those of the Cullen Bank and Trust. Richard Kardys, now head of Frost's Financial Management Group (which includes the Trust Department), describes those assets as "almost unbelievable for a bank just eight years old. It's rare for a small bank to start with a trust department from Day One. The Cullen Bank had done that. The department was created just to handle the assets of the Cullen family and the R. E. ('Bob') Smith families, which were plenty big enough for a whole trust department." Today, according to Houston/Galveston Regional President Dave Beck, that department's assets approach $600 million.

"When I started here in 1976," says Kardys, "people set up trusts to look after family assets and reduce taxes for their children. Trusts for money management, market investments, organizations, businesses, and pension funds got big later on. But we still think of our trust department as a family enterprise. We watch whole generations grow up, grow old, and die. We watch new generations take their place. It's as if we're part of those families ourselves."

No area of the bank reflects the Frost tradition of treating every customer with courtesy, friendliness, and respect more than the Trust Department does. Says one Frost trust officer, "We never judge anybody by their appearance or mannerisms when they walk in here. We know better. Even if someone is seedy, or unshaven, or dressed like an unfortunate homeless person, he might be here to create a trust with some huge sum of money or stock certificates or Treasury instruments he's got salted away at home in a coffee can or a book or a drawer. We've seen it happen. People fitting that description have walked in here carrying so much cash, just the interest on it could have made them millionaires."

chapter 5

The Twilight of the Seventies: 1978–1979

As the decade approached its close, the bank had taken further strides in the field of technology. Year after year throughout the Seventies, its cutting-edge innovations had beaten many other banks to the punch. Top market position hinged on Frost's ability to offer the smorgasbord of services (including state-of-the-art technology) impersonal megabanks did while also offering the relationship banking they did not. That ability guaranteed the Frost customer the advantages of both a large urban bank and a small community bank without the disadvantages of either.

The Seventies saw the advent of Frost Telephone Banking—an automated audio system by which depositors could phone in for balance or other account information: By simply dialing the bank and entering an account number, they could utilize the system to get the desired information. It was the decade of the Microfiche, by which the bank was able to store vast amounts of data from informational reports onto a small sheet of microfilm, eliminating the need for tons of paperwork piled in warehouses. On one fiche could be stored all the data contained in 205 sheets of paper.

On-line Teller Terminals allowed a teller to bring up a customer's account "on-line" (via computer terminal) and determine instantly whether that customer had funds enough on hand to cover a check or withdrawal. And with the mid-Seventies came sophisticated fine tuning of the MICR Capture: an ingenious device, introduced in the late Sixties, which read the magnetic information on a check and stored it in a computer. The Capture soon became equipped with a "3890 Reader-Sorter"— a 30-foot-long robotic device, right out of *Star Wars*, that captured the information on 2000 checks per minute, photographed it onto microfilm for internal purposes, and then sorted the checks into appropriate pockets for further activity. Later, in the early Nineties, photographed images of the checks would be mailed to account holders instead of the checks themselves.

At the March 1977 Board meeting, plans were hatched to invest in two more new computer systems and in additional state-of-the-art "on-line" terminals. Primary Check Processing, also implemented in 1977, was an instant mechanism enabling anyone (having security clearance) within the organization to look into checking accounts, for debit and credit information, on a computer terminal; potentially, it put every bank employee "on-line."

"ATMs," or Automated Teller Machines, arrived at the end of the decade. Frost was one of the first Texas banks to install them. Originally, all ATMs were located inside the bank, for impatient customers who needed cash in a matter of seconds. Soon, however, with an amendment to that part of the Texas Constitution proscribing "branch banking," they appeared, with enhanced service capabilities, in motor banks, supermarkets, shopping malls, hospitals, theater lobbies, and many other places.

"Without those innovations," says retired Senior Vice-President Frank Sievers, who installed Frost's very first computer in 1963, "our Seventies customers might have left us for bigger banks. Technology

96

was a continuing process that allowed us to compete and to enhance our reputation. By this time, our data processing center, which we'd bought from Bob Guthrie in the late Sixties, was processing for almost a hundred smaller banks throughout South Texas. To those banks, *we* were one of the 'bigger banks.'

"It's a misconception," Sievers adds, "that Seventies automation cost people jobs. It may have kept us from hiring more people, but it also created jobs that didn't exist before. In the long run, it benefited everybody."

The Seventies ended on a high note for Cullen/Frost Bankers, Inc. and a low note for the nation. Yet even that high note rang slightly false, as though heralding a more troublesome decade ahead.

The decade in its twilight would go down in American history as the era in which the wave of postwar prosperity finally crested and commenced to recede. Recession had followed recession. Inflation was rampant: a legacy of the improvident "guns-and-butter" policies of the Sixties. Wages doubled, yet Americans felt they were falling behind. They were. The decade's inflation rate—100 percent—meant that after adjusting for taxes, workers took home fewer real dollars in 1979 than in 1970.

In 1978, President Jimmy Carter named a conservative banker, Paul A. Volcker, to chair the Federal Reserve Board. Volcker's method of checking inflation—limiting the growth the money supply—was draconian and unpopular. The Federal Reserve adopted a "tight money" policy that further heightened interest rates, made borrowing even tougher, and spread the general malaise.

Things got worse in 1979, when the OPEC Arab countries, inflamed by anti-American revolution in Iran, doubled oil prices again. Soon Americans were paying over a dollar—the most ever—for a gallon of gas. The long lines and allocation programs of 1974 were revived. Higher oil prices meant higher prices for everything made from petroleum or with petroleum-powered machinery. By Christmas 1979, the American economy was a shambles.

The Texas economy, conversely, was a profits windfall. With renewed dependence on domestic hydrocarbon fuels, the Oil Patch boomed louder than ever; with one-third of the nation's hydrocarbon reserves, Texas was a country unto itself; one late-Seventies TV commercial dubbed Lone Star, a San Antonio brew, "The National Beer of Texas."

"We were fat and sassy while the rest of the world was suffering," remembers Frost Jr., though oil-blessed Mexico, for all its internal problems, was not doing so badly either. As Texas prospered, so did its banks. Texas had become the fourth largest banking market in the country. From 1976 to 1977 alone, its bank deposits grew by 11.5 percent: the highest increase among the 10 leading states. Texas boasted three of the nation's 10 largest cities, with Cullen/Frost a solid presence in each; one of those cities, Houston, was the nation's petroleum capital.

Nevertheless, black clouds loomed on the state's banking horizon. With runaway inflation, soaring interest rates, and restrictive monetary policy in the forecast, how many OPEC price hikes could Texas banks hope for? The late Seventies had witnessed disturbing trends that could make life tougher in the Eighties. Insurance companies, securities firms, and thrifts soon would encroach on domains traditionally reserved for banks; regulatory reins were loosening on every financial institution except banks.

As early as September 1977, the Board, perhaps smelling trouble, was discussing ways to increase capitalization. In a 1979 newspaper interview, Frost Bank President Corky Sledge warned that banks "could be headed toward paying interest on all categories of deposits very soon" and that "greater proportions of our source of funds will become interest-bearing. That won't break our system. But it will force us to manage ourselves differently if we are to protect the assets of our depositors and make a profit for our stockholders." It had a portentous ring. Was Sledge just talking about modernizing management, or was he hinting that to survive in an exploding field of competitors, his bank might have to implement radical changes for which its traditions had not prepared it?

Even old reliable D. Ansley was skittish, chomping at the bit. Though its numbers were respectable (at year-end 1979, it serviced $205.63 million in mortgage loans for San Antonio, Corpus Christi, and the Rio Grande Valley), it was hobbled by tight money and restrictive policy and unfree to avail itself of the regulatory easings of the late Seventies. Why? Because it was owned by a bank. A conservative tradition-bound bank, at that.

Still, there was—or seemed—cause to rejoice. Texas would always have its oil fields, would it not? And the Eighties would vote into Washington a fresh Administration, flush with optimism, that was not only pro-business and anti-regulation but capable of lifting the nation's dispirited morale and wrenching inflation to its knees. Now was the twilight of the Seventies, and soon it would be morning in America. But would Texas, whose economic fortunes always seemed to mirror the nation's in reverse, share in the glory of that morning?

chapter 6

Good Times, Galveston, and the Kempner Merger: 1980–1982

For Cullen/Frost Bankers, Inc. and the communities it served, the first three years of the Eighties were good years. Who could hear that time bomb ticking up the road? They were years when Texas continued to shine; TV's most avidly watched show was "Dallas"; newcomers with new money poured into the state, the fastest growing in the Union after Florida. Giddy and flush with success, Texas did not know that its joyride was a roller coaster.

San Antonio's building frenzy of the late Seventies gave no sign of a slowdown either, as the city took on a strikingly new appearance. Skyscrapers and hotel towers transformed the downtown skyline. New office buildings and business parks lined the North Side freeways. San Antonio was looking like the big city it yearned to be.

CFBI continued on its fast track of expansion. Board minutes for the July 1980 meeting, for example, document a resolution to acquire a credit life insurance company. Bank credit life insurance is a supplemental loan benefit by which, if a customer dies while borrowing to finance a house or automobile, his policy credits the balance of his loan. In 1981, Cullen/Frost created a credit life subsidiary, C/F Life Insurance Company, which began operating in January 1982, and a general insurance agency subsidiary, Daltex General Agency, Inc.

In 1981 also, plans were announced for a 600,000-square-foot Two Frost Tower, the largest high-rise office building in the city's history, to be constructed due north of the existing Tower, with a graceful open plaza of green space connecting. It was a sublime vision destined to remain just that: For reasons explained further on, Two Frost Tower was never built.

The same year saw significant enhancements to the leadership group. Corky Sledge became Frost Bank Board chairman, Fred Lepick Frost Bank president, and Tom Frost Jr. (who began a three-year term that year on the Federal Reserve Advisory Council) was elected senior Board chairman. Lepick was a formidable but intensely likable attorney whose wealth of common sense compensated for the lack of much banking experience; Sledge was a people person, a diplomat, a skilled personnel manager gifted with charm and charisma; crucially, the changes freed up Frost Jr. to grow the holding company.

Grow it he did. In January 1982, Cullen/Frost's fifth San Antonio bank and third *de novo*, North Frost, opened in the thriving Northeast sector. It would set San Antonio first-year banking records, ending 1982 with $27 million in deposits. And in June 1982, Cullen/Frost entered its fifth major metropolitan but sixth overall market—flourishing high-tech Austin—by acquiring 10-year-old Chase National Bank in the city's booming north-central sector. The little bank's year-end-1982 deposits were only $34 million, but they were growing by 10 percent annually.

The acquisition was advantageous for other reasons, too. The bank's shareholders were major players in Austin community growth; among them was the family of the late President Lyndon B. Johnson.

The move furthered Frost's tradition of forging alliances with personages for whom community development was a priority second to none.

The Kempners were such people—an acculturated Jewish family in Galveston, the kind about whom epic novels are written and movies made. In 1902, they had acquired control of Galveston's ailing, state-chartered, 31-year-old Island City Savings Bank, which was later renamed the United States National Bank. And now, 80 years later, in 1982, their bank would be merged with the Cullen/Frost holding company.

Boasting deposits of $113 million and a bountiful trust department, the USNB was Galveston's second largest bank. Also merged was the Kempners' Sugar Land State Bank (in a town, 25 miles from downtown Houston, where the Kempners owned the Imperial Sugar Company refinery); its deposits totaled $46 million.

The Kempner family history was fascinating. Like the Cullens', it bore astonishing parallels to the Frost history. In 1854, as a teenager, the patriarch Harris Kempner had fled Russian Poland to escape anti-Semitism and conscription in the Czar's army. After working as a construction laborer in the American Northeast, he had gone to Texas, as had Colonel T. C. Frost, with a heart lusting for adventure. Also like the Colonel, he served as a Confederate soldier during the Civil War, then returned from that war to make his fortune in the mercantile business.

The town where he chose to make that fortune was Galveston, then the busiest Texas port; there, he made his first million as a cotton factor and wholesale merchant. Though a prototype of the rags-to-riches 19th Century entrepreneur, Harris Kempner was (again like Colonel Frost) known for his scrupulously ethical business practices all his life. Death claimed him in 1894. Whereupon Harris's eldest son, Isaac Herbert ("Ike"), left Washington and Lee University in Virginia to oversee the family business and care for his mother and seven siblings. (He eventually graduated and took a law degree.) Part of the family business—H. Kempner, as it was called, which he ran for 75 years—was the Island City Savings Bank. His father had been its president. On summer vacations, as a star-struck boy, Ike had a ringside seat while Harris conducted hefty transactions with big-shot, cigar-smoking New York bankers.

In 1923, H. Kempner trustees financed a high-rise building, Galveston's tallest, for the bank. But banking was a sideline for the Kempners, who had expanded their fortune with enterprises like real estate, paper and furniture manufacture, international trade, wholesale grocering, barges, railroads, insurance, and sugar refining, the field in which they had transformed Sugar Land, Texas, from a shanty convict-labor operation into a model company town.

As a prominent "Islander Family," the Kempners were passionately devoted to Galveston. After the Great Storm of 1900, Ike, by then a local politician, directed relief efforts and planned the Galveston Sea Wall. During World War I, he was Galveston's mayor. Devotion to the community was his legacy to his son, Harris L. ("Bush") Kempner (1903-1987) and his grandson, Harris L. ("Shrub") Kempner Jr., born in 1940. To this day, the family generously supports orphanages, charities, public and parochial schools, student loan programs, refuges, and a local hospital for the indigent.

Like the Frosts, the Kempners maintained a business tradition of "family cohesion." (One Kempner, Lee, worked his way up from bank trainee to president.) Like the Frosts, they confronted problems promptly and squarely, before they could get out of hand. Their reputation for philosophical consistency and loyalty to employees equaled that of the Frosts and Cullens.

The merger was chiefly negotiated by Bush Kempner a few years before his death. Says his son Shrub, "We were in no trouble at the time. We'd made some bad real estate loans but come out of them after a scrubbing period, so we were clean as any bank in the state. We merged with the Cullens and Frosts because we knew that with them, our past could be preserved. If questions arose about our bank's role in the Galveston community, they would understand our position better than some megabank that didn't know our history. Comfort was a factor."

For Cullen/Frost, there were bigger factors than comfort. According to its 1981 annual report, USNB and Sugar Land State Bank assets would boost the Houston-area total to $796 million. The Sugar Land addition would extend CFBI's Houston market southward. And the merger would bring in USNB's time-honored, community-venerated trust department.

In July 1982, the Board elected Bush and Shrub Kempner as advisory directors; earlier, it had granted their request that the USNB retain its name, making it unique among CFBI banks. "Once your name is lost, you can't replace it," argued the Kempners, and their bank was one of the last in the country granted a "United States National" appellation. (The corporation was wise to make an exception. During the storm at sea from 1983 to 1991, the USNB would be the only ship in its fleet to turn a profit every year.) At this writing in 1998, Cullen/Frost remains a two-bank holding company consisting of Frost Bank and Galveston's United States National.

Greater-than-ever support of Galveston community projects followed on the heels of the Kempner merger. In 1983, the USNB financed rebuilding efforts in the devastated wake of Hurricane Alicia. From 1984 to 1989, it was the leading lender for the city's Downtown Revitalization Committee rehabilitation projects and for new buildings in Galveston's "Boomtown" section. Recalls F. A. ("Andy") Odom, the current USNB president who had worked at the Houston Cullen bank before being dispatched to Galveston in 1982, "Borrowers willing to revitalize downtown got reduced rates if they qualified. We led in the amount of money loaned to those borrowers."

The bank also helped finance construction of a four-story downtown parking garage and a hotel on the beachfront; and it supported tourism with funds to bring the restored 1877 Scottish sailing ship *Elissa* to the Port of Galveston as a museum of 19th Century maritime history. In so doing, it was faithful to community traditions of the Kempners, Cullens, and Frosts alike.

Back at the home front, there was good news and bad. The early Eighties saw San Antonio officially designated a Foreign Trade Zone: This made it the two-way distribution point for a wide variety of wholesale goods bound for either South Texas or Mexico. The bad news was that the 1982 devaluation of the peso, coupled with exchange controls imposed by the Mexican government and a move to nationalize Mexican banks, delivered a blow to both San Antonio and Texas markets along the border. It impacted Frost directly, too, because it resulted in the termination of a pending arrangement to acquire the Union Bank of Laredo.

Nevertheless, the Frost Bank International Department's relationship with Mexico was a win-win proposition. In the words of Richard W. Evans Jr., the current Frost CEO in 1998, "Mexico's internal problems actually bolstered our liquidity. When Mexican nationals took money out of their banks, they deposited it in ours. When they took it out of our bank to invest in their country, they facilitated U. S.-Mexico trade: our primary objective.

"During the Eighties," Evans continues, "while other Texas banks suffered deposit losses, ours showed increases. Deposits from Mexico helped us maintain capital. Even in our worst years, we provided lines of credit to Mexican banks."

Frost Bank also said good-bye to an old friend in 1982: its D. Ansley mortgage subsidiary. As mentioned earlier, regulatory easings had opened the door for mortgage companies to become equity partners in their lending projects so long as such companies were not owned by a bank. But D. Ansley was owned by a bank. Later in the Eighties, banks themselves could become such equity partners—but Frost Bank was unwilling to lend and borrow on the same project, a questionable practice which violated its traditions.

Frost Bank had great affection for D. Ansley and its president, John C. ("Johnny") Webbles, and loyalty to its friends was a strong tradition. "We wanted Johnny free to do everything his competitors could," says 41-year-old Don Frost, the current market president for Northeast San Antonio and the third-born of Frost Jr.'s four sons. "But as a subsidiary of our bank, he was handcuffed. We sold D. Ansley back to him and financed the transaction. They're a pure mortgage banker again—and good customers of ours to this day."

For Texas banks, the early Eighties were an era of rapid growth. With the Kempner merger, the number of Cullen/Frost banks reached double digits. More expansion soon followed. Board minutes for the April 1981 meeting record a motion to charter a *de novo* Cullen Bank/City West in Houston. Located in a $2.2 billion development at Westheimer and West Belt, Cullen Bank/City West opened in 1983 with an initial capitalization of $4 million. Also that year, the company bought Houston's Northfield National Bank, chartered years earlier by a Robertson member of the Cullen Family and renamed Cullen Bank Northfield. Its deposits were just $16 million, but it stood in Houston's fastest-growing area. For a variety of reasons, the company later closed down this bank.

Five banks now served Houston/Galveston, the biggest CFBI market. But in size, the Cullen/Frost expansions did not rival those of certain other, bigger Texas bank holding companies. "The bigger they come, the harder they fall," went the cliche. But what did cliches know?

chapter 7

Reversal of Fortune: 1983–1985

The wise men of industry have a saying: Often the best deals are the ones you do not make. In July 1983, heady with optimism, Cullen/Frost agreed to merge with Houston-based First City Bancorporation of Texas, Inc., the state's fourth largest bank holding company. If consummated, this alliance would create the second largest bank holding company in Texas and one of the 20 largest in America: a merger so colossal that the Frost name itself would be relinquished in the bargain. Bigness, however, was not the objective; the reason the move was even considered was the changing regulatory environment.

How would Mr. Joe have viewed the relinquishing of names? No more Frost Bank? No more Cullen/Frost Bankers, Inc.? What was going on? "It was the worst call of my career," Tom Frost Jr. laments. "I was doing the wrong thing for the right reasons."

As those reasons, he cites the following: (1) both holding companies and the Texas market were economically healthy at the time; (2)

First City operated a robust 65 banking subsidiaries, spread out over 17 Texas markets; (3) the merger would give Cullen/Frost a dominant downtown presence and a huge trust department in the flourishing Austin market (where it had just the suburban Chase bank) and pave the way for further Austin expansion; (4) the First City organization, headed up by J. A. ("Jim") Elkins, Jr., embraced values consistent with the Frost, Kempner, and Cullen philosophies. "We would've become First City," Tom Frost Jr. admits. "And I would've been responsible for all banking operations outside of Houston."

He also cites a fifth motive. The merger, a precaution, provided for self-defense. Frost Jr. had seen the future, and it was a dread juggernaut of Goliathan bank holding companies like Citicorp and Chase Manhattan crossing state lines and gobbling up banks in Texas. The merger would give the holding company muscle to ward off an invasion already underway in other parts of the country. Deregulation was the shibboleth of the regime in Washington; the big banks were coming; a First City merger might ensure a Frost Bank survival.

Fortunately, as things turned out, the merger never happened.

One reason it never happened was the unforeseen plunge in oil prices, later in 1983, from $39 a barrel to $26. For Texas banks, the drop had the sound of a sickening thud. An alarmed Federal Reserve slowed mergers to a virtual halt. As oil prices foundered, so did exploration and loan demand. Banks were saddled with loans from the Boom years that turned into problems. Many would look to real estate loans for compensation—a desperate move, as things transpired, like swimming from the *Titanic* to the *Bismarck*, were such a feat possible within the limits of time and space.

Plummeting oil prices hit the Texas Oil Patch—Midland, Houston, Corpus Christi—not just first but hardest. Though the stricken areas comprised less than a fourth of Cullen/Frost business, the corporation sustained a 1983 net loss of $22 million, or $3.16 per common share: its worst beating to date. "Why didn't you see this coming?" one bank examiner scolded Frost Jr. "It's your job." The banker good-naturedly replied, "Why didn't you? It's your job too."

Actually, had he been looking for it, Frost Jr. might have seen it coming. There had been signs. The slump began late in 1981 and continued through 1982. The cause? Overproduction—a market glut. The "energy shortage" scare of the Carter years had created an hysterical urgency to shore up reserves and lessen U. S. dependence on foreign oil. Even banks as conservative as Frost had expanded loans for domestic exploration. Some banks' loan-to-deposit ratios had soared past 100 percent.

But "foreign oil" had turned the tables. Forgotten, or overlooked, was the fact that OPEC had been keeping oil prices unnaturally high since its 1973 oil embargo. Before it, oil had been selling for $3.50 per barrel; eight years later, that figure had increased tenfold and the Texas slice of the energy pie had grown from $4.5 billion to $45 billion per year. By 1981, the state was producing one-third of the oil the United States consumed. But the world price was ever subject to the whims of Arab sheiks and princes. If they could confound the West by raising oil prices, they could also confound it by cutting them.

In 1982, as the nation fell into another recession, Texas was still riding high. But in 1983, as the nation emerged from its recession, Texas fell into one. At the height of Texas energy overactivity, the Arabs, weary of punishing the West with curtailed production and propped-up prices, decided to let their own spigots gush. Abruptly, they cut prices by a third. It was as if the Lone Star State were the ground zero of a nuclear attack. On Wall Street, the ecological slogan "Don't Mess with Texas" took on the meaning of a financial caveat.

It could be argued that Texas banks, like Humpty Dumpty, had set themselves up for a fall. With the Eighties, they had become too growth-oriented for their own good. Their stocks were the darlings of Wall Street touts; CFBI stock, for example, had soared past $25 per share. Performance, the name of the game, was measured by profits, and Texas banks were under the gun from outside investors to turn a profit every quarter.

Fortunately, just the same, Cullen/Frost refused to lend—even on energy projects—to people with whom it had no prior relationship or did not know; refused to be a "transactional" lender, with no regard to the borrowers involved, merely because energy production or exploration was the objective; refused to escalate its projections on oil prices even when current prices were sky-high and Midland banks escalating them to $80 a barrel. Unfortunately, it did escalate its projections for oil-field equipment loans, which turned sour as smart, conservative production loans managed to hold their own.

Even relationship banking has its pitfalls; many tried-and-true Cullen/Frost customers were hopelessly overinvested in energy; loans made to them for the best of reasons were bad loans, mistakes that had to be corrected. As was its tradition, the bank was quick to confront those problems proactively, before they got out of hand. Board minutes for its 1983 meeting show the company charging off bad loans and building up reserves to an extent even greater than bank examiners required. They also indicate that it stopped paying dividends to itself from its Houston Cullen bank (whose 1983 net income was a negative $22.48 million) and that it replaced a dividend taken from the bank earlier in the year.

Even more drastic measures were required—and fast. Cullen/Frost also responded with tough management changes involving crack troubleshooters. From its Dallas Citizens National Bank, it dispatched the president, J. Gordon Muir Jr., to the Houston Cullen bank, where he oversaw a virtual recapitalization. From its San Antonio Frost Bank, it dispatched Board Vice-Chairman Clyde Crews to Corpus Christi to re-capitalize the Parkdale operation. The overnight reassignments had the air of a military alert.

Crews recalls, "I rented an apartment in Corpus. I'd go down every Sunday and come back to San Antonio on Friday. We'd seen influential directors leave Parkdale for Corpus Christi's International Bank because of an age-limit rule. When the International Bank got sold, I had to convince 'em to come back and help us recapitalize. I got the rule changed; the old guys went back to Parkdale; the bank's been solid ever since."

Another company outpost in 1983 trouble was Austin's recently acquired Chase National Bank, renamed Frost Bank North Austin in 1985. The energy contagion had not hit Austin yet; the bank was simply suffering from everyday, garden-variety bad loans. This time, the doctor on house call was R. E. ("Buster") Fawcett Jr., a senior executive vice-president and loan specialist at the San Antonio bank and a longtime friend of Tom Frost Jr.'s before coming to work there. Fawcett quickly implemented the Frost systems of rigid adherence to conservative loan policy and relationship banking at Chase National. As usual, the system worked. "As for the problem loans," he recalls, "I charged off some and collected the others. That took care of that." For all its headaches, the Austin bank closed out the bleak year $273,000 in the black. Fawcett would perform similar troubleshooting feats at the company's Portland State Bank, in the Coastal Bend area, a few years later.

The swift remedies illustrate not just the bank's traditional ability to move personnel around (rather than conscript "specialists" from the outside) during times of crisis but also the versatility and mobility of Frost management troubleshooters, who could pack up and head for other cities at a moment's notice. The man doing the most traveling at the time, however, was Tom Frost Jr. himself—visiting ailing banks and putting together the First City merger simultaneously. Flying Southwest Airlines to Dallas one day, Houston the next, and other Texas cities as needed, he threatened long-standing Frequent Flyer records and became part of a crisis management-passenger subculture. Another objective of his travels was to cheer his people up, reassure them that everything would be all right, and keep the team together: an effort he would have to repeat three years later during another crisis.

He also flew to New York—to arrange lines of credit from supporting banks in case of a run by depositors who might deem the situation worse than it was. "We never had to use those lines for that reason," he says, "but it was reassuring to have them."

The 1983 Texas banking debacle could be chalked up to bad timing. Overconfidence in the state economy, domestic energy overproduction, overaggressive lending practices, OPEC price cutting, and financial-industry deregulation all coincided at an unfortuitous point. There was confusion and sometimes chaos.

Deregulation, which banks had cried out for in the Seventies, ironically made it harder for them to slam on the brakes and shift from growth to crisis management when the collapsing energy market veered out of control. In 1981, product and price deregulation had authorized interest-bearing checking and money market accounts, giving banks the opportunity to compete with money market mutual funds; late in 1982, these instruments allowed banks to pay interest rates greater than those permitted on regular savings accounts; also in 1982, S&Ls, formerly restricted to home loans, were (1) granted extravagantly permissive lending powers, (2) allowed to engage in the same speculative commercial-real-estate ventures banks were, and (3) even permitted to own interest in the ventures they made loans for. And 1983 saw the end of interest rate ceilings on consumer time deposits at banks and thrifts.

With so much sweeping change to adjust to, the last thing Texas banking needed was a precipitous drop in energy prices. It got one anyway. Meanwhile, geographic deregulation, yet another change, was paving the road to interstate banking. State boundaries were disappearing. Technology had created instant financial delivery systems such that distances measured by thousands of miles posed no delay. Every week confronted banking with new outside competitors, free to intrude upon any area formerly reserved for banks they wished to.

Certain deregulatory "advances" profited competitors of banks more than they did banks themselves—and pressured banks to implement them whether they wanted to or not. Yet one Frost executive recalls, "A number of banks didn't, but we actually supported product, price, and geographic deregulation. We had to offer these new services. Not to would have left us behind the field of competition in a cloud of dust. But it happened at a time when caution and deliberation and conservatism might have profited us more."

It also happened at a time when boundaries between bank and nonbank financial services were blurring. Despite the uncertainty and confusion, banks could benefit from that. New regulations in 1983, for example, allowed Frost Bank to create a discount brokerage department for trading stocks and bonds.

It was a major step, long overdue. "As far back as the Fifties," recalls a veteran Frost executive, "we could buy and sell securities for you if you didn't have a brokerage account and didn't want one. Many small investors didn't. You could bring your stock certificate in and we'd sell your stock through our own brokerage account—on an unsolicited basis—without charging you a fee. We'd just credit your account when the money arrived." In 1974, the bank established a "Bond Department," later called "Investment Services," to perform such transactions more officially. And now, in 1983, with a bona fide discount brokerage, the buying and selling would become formalized.

Still, this conservative bank stopped short of actually soliciting investors and offering investment advice for a while longer. Three years later, in March 1986, the holding company formed a subsidiary, Frost Brokerage Services Inc., to streamline transactions related to the sale and purchase of securities of all types. But the subsidiary served primarily to execute unsolicited trades for six more years, until 1992, when regulatory prohibitions eased and the corporation amended its business plan to permit the offering of advice and the active soliciting of trades.

As of 1983, however, investment activity was simply more specialized. Explains Discount Brokerage President Karen Banks, "Our new department focused on stocks, corporate bonds, IRAs, and mutual funds. But our Investment Services continued to specialize in municipal bonds, commercial paper, treasury securities, and repurchase agreements." Once more, turn-about was fair play. If securities firms could encroach on banking, banking could return the favor—and lure investors with added convenience, speed, product specialization, and the security only a bank could offer.

On occasion, one Frost Bank tradition (such as flexibility) has conflicted with another (such as conservatism), and officers have had to take sides. Predictably, at a bank like Frost whose traditional roles were rigidly defined, aggressive investment solicitation was not unanimously popular when finally allowed in 1992. The debate was vocal as to whether Frost should simply encourage customers to put their money into the bank rather than into money market mutual funds.

"But," Frost Jr. says today, "we had to offer the choice. Our officers could decide whether to encourage deposits or encourage investments. Some customers were going to pull their money out of the bank and invest it anyway. Why not invest it through us?"

Having lived through the Crash of 1983, Cullen/Frost, the state's eighth largest holding company, prayed that its worst days were behind it. They were not. But for two years, the corporation did enjoy a mild recovery.

Its 1984 annual report showed it back in the profits column, with a positive net income of $15.149 million; provision for loan loss was down to $13.532 million from 1983's stratospheric $66.493 million; deposits and assets had grown by 10 percent since 1983, loans by 15 percent. A healthy expansion was continuing. And fortunately, hard-hit Houston, with no offense to the Bayou City intended, housed just four Cullen/Frost banks and just 16 percent of Cullen/Frost assets going into 1985.

"Actually, our Houston Cullen operation had performed extremely well between the merger in 1977 and the first oil bust in 1983," Houston/Galveston Regional President Dave Beck points out today. "But it had made too many loans for oil production and energy services. Its crises were the earliest of all the Frost banks. But it was also the first to come out of them."

For Texas, it marked the end of an era: Oil prices would never again soar as high as they had in 1981, and borrowers and investors knew it. Perniciously, many would look to long-term commercial real estate for compensation. So powerful was the real estate magnet that many successful professionals quit their jobs to jump into the field. Even banks felt the pull. In 1984, the State Finance Commission approved plans by the Texas Department of Banking to seek legislative authority for state-chartered banks to "invest in real estate for development purposes." Hapless thrifts invested in real estate development too. Many banks began making wildly speculative real estate loans to recoup their losses from disastrous energy loans they had made. Many thrifts, having "borrowed short and lent long" before interest rates shot up in the late Seventies, took a frantic "transaction-oriented" approach to loan-making (as did a good number of banks) with no concern about the parties involved. Their timing could not have been worse.

According to the company's financial accounting, just the Houston Cullen and the Dallas bank had suffered 1983 losses—and the latter only because it had purchased oil-and-gas participations from the San Antonio bank, which had earlier purchased them from the First

National Bank of Midland. In truth, however, the overall damage had been far worse. And the 1984 rebound was deceptive, lending the impression that the disaster had been a fluke.

It had not. The following year saw company profits head south again. For Texas banks, 1985 was a horror; the State Department of Banks reported 12 financial institutions, with assets of $400 million, closing during the year, doubling the total for 1984. Cullen/Frost's net income dipped by almost $5 million, to $10.3 million.

Nineteen-eighty-five was not all bad, however. The holding company's net charge-offs for bad loans were $6.831 million less than the previous year's, with energy accounting for 63 percent of the total and real estate credits for just 9 percent. Energy-industry loans comprised just 6.9 percent of the total portfolio. By year-end 1985, oil prices had risen by $4 per barrel—to $30—from 1983's nadir. "Energy industry recovery seems imminent," chortled the financial page of one San Antonio daily newspaper. But things were not what they seemed.

Nineteen-eighty-five was also the year of a Cullen/Frost disappointment which turned out to be a blessing in disguise. In March, with no indication that regulatory approval would be forthcoming in the 20th Century, the First City merger was officially called off after two years of "pending" status. What had happened? The problem was what had not. Explained one Frost executive, "The Fed never said No to the merger but never said Yes either. It hemmed and hawed until both sides made a joint decision not to go through with it."

For Cullen/Frost, this bitter pill of disappointment proved good medicine for a couple of reasons: (1) since the merger's announcement, First City had been burdened by problems which ultimately would crush it; and (2) 1985 was no time for a merger with any Texas bank. Often the best deals are those you do not make.

A Cullen/Frost Board member in Houston noted, "Fortunately, the regulators really did their job." But the holding company's involvement with hapless First City was not over. In the Nineties, it would be resurrected.

◆ ◆ ◆

When Corky Sledge took early retirement in 1985, Tom Frost Jr. returned as Frost Bank Board chairman, and the directors elected Robert S. McClane president of the holding company. Dick Evans became bank president, replacing Fred Lepick, who became Frost Bank Board vice-chairman and Trust Committee chairman. McClane and Evans reorganized bank functions, with Evans heading up lending and customer relations and McClane in charge of operations and the financial area. Additionally, Kenneth A. Trapp was promoted to executive vice-president, and Phillip D. Green, a senior vice-president since 1983, became Cullen/Frost treasurer.

It was strategic reorganizing, designed to answer the merciless challenges of the Eighties. Lending was Evans's forte—he had been chief loan officer—and now the bank presidency required increased attention to credit. McClane's managerial skills as a staff overseer of the big picture qualified him to ride herd over the holding company and to bolster its staying power and capital. The Trust Department bulwark, whose common stock funds were eventually to outperform the S&P 500, would be ably assisted by Trust Committee oversight and by the talents of an attorney like Lepick, who as president had excelled as a manager and dealt capably with customers one on one. Green—a Longview, Texas, native—had distinguished himself in the financial area since joining the bank in 1980. And with expansion on the back burner, Tom Frost Jr. was again needed at his command post as the bank's Board chairman.

There were further "inside moves" as well. In 1985, Evans and McClane formed the Corporate Management Committee, which was to function as a vehicle for bringing together the company's key executives. Besides Frost Jr., Evans, and McClane, Committtee members included Kenneth A. Trapp, J. Gordon Muir Jr., Citizens National Bank of Dallas President Robert T. Huthnance, and (a little later) Phillip D. Green.

The San Antonio bank, Cullen/Frost's home-field superstar, continued to be the player that carried the team. Throughout the decade, it would prove a fountain of recapitalization for Cullen/Frost banks dying of thirst. Its success mirrored the vigorous growth of the city during the early Eighties. From 1980 to 1985, San Antonio's population grew by 8.3 percent, making it the nation's 10th largest city. Frost Bank led its commercial banking market, with 23.1 percent of deposits. Sixty-six percent of Cullen/Frost assets were concentrated in San Antonio.

Bad times would soon come to the city. But the holding company was blessed with luck that the Eighties plague did not afflict all its cities at once. Still, San Antonio had cause for concern as early as 1985. With 2.7 million square feet of commercial real estate and office space ready for occupancy, it had but 1.2 million of it absorbed: a dangerous ratio. Yet nobody worried. Why should they? Throughout the early Eighties, San Antonio had been on a growth-and-development trip, and the guru was its handsome supermayor, Henry Cisneros, who had taken office in 1981 and would serve four consecutive terms.

This charismatic Mexican American from the city's West Side had finally bridged the gap between the Anglo and Hispanic communities. His greatest contribution was the forging of a sense of civic unity stronger than the city had ever known before. Not only had the shift to district representation and the accompanying surge of minority political influence played a part, but in the broader community Henry Cisneros embodied a change of attitude that crossed traditional lines and created unlikely alliances. The excitement generated was palpable and electric.

HemisFair had attracted movers and shakers to San Antonio who stayed around to give the city an economic face-lift. Cisneros was the leader they had waited a dozen years for. Though a Democrat, he was the ideal mayor for the Reagan Eighties. Soon people all over the country were hearing about the dynamic young *Latino* mayor who saw economic development, personal initiative, and new jobs as the salvation of a city with a per capita income of $5,672 at the close of the

Seventies. Working with the Chambers, the EDF, and organizations like United San Antonio and Target '90, Cisneros became the greatest salesman San Antonio had ever had.

In 1981, the EDF lured 3900 new jobs to Cisnerostown; 1100 others were created the same year without its help. The EDF figure dropped to 500 in 1982 but rose to 850 in 1983. In 1984, Isotronics Inc. of Massachusetts announced it would establish a $200 million plant in San Antonio; Harcourt Brace Jovanovich Inc, the nation's largest textbook publisher, trumpeted plans for an $8 million plant on the West Side, which Cisneros finalized with a trip to HBJ's Florida offices; the following year, the city landed the coveted aquatic park Sea World and the thriving H-E-B grocery chain's corporate headquarters.

Building and redevelopment continued to boom. Steps were taken for a Vista Verde South Mall, Plaza del Rio (downtown) Mall, Fiesta Plaza Mall on the West Side, and the belated redevelopment of HemisFair Plaza. In 1985, Marriott announced plans for a downtown 1000-room Rivercenter Hotel; Sheraton planned a 950-room hotel near HemisFair Plaza; and the tony downtown 177-room Emily Morgan Hotel went up on Houston Street. By the summer of 1985, the city had 1477 more hotel rooms than a year earlier—a 10 percent gain—as the total ballooned to 15,500. New hotels along the freeways sported names like Wyndham, Holiday Inn Northwest, Embassy Suites, AmeriSuites, Drury Inn, and Hampton Inn.

Frost Bank financed many of those projects, hotels included, even as its loan policies tightened and its focus narrowed on the holding company's problems. Downtown was still its favorite place, and it was ceaselessly active there, with a new emphasis given to apartment dwellings. The bank's activity also extended, beyond new construction, to salvaging and renovating grand, historic structures downtown. In 1983, itself cramped for space, it renovated the old Rand Building, its next-door neighbor, and began a three-phase move-in. Meanwhile, the venerable Frost Bank Building on Main Plaza, built in the Twenties, was purchased by the city and forever saved from the wrecker's ball.

The bank also involved itself in the new Texas Research and Technology Foundation—Tom Frost Jr. was a founding board member—which would build the vital Texas Research Park in the far Northwest sector. In 1984, when the city lost out to Austin for a prestigious Microelectronic and Computer Corporation (MCC) research center, Mayor Cisneros had decided that San Antonio's industrial future lay in biomedical, not computer, technology. One result of that decision was a costly feasibility study, partially financed by Frost Bank, for a biotechnology research park as the setting for such a future.

"We weren't prime movers in the Texas Research Park," says Frost Jr. today, "the way we'd been for HemisFair and the Medical Center. But we did pitch in with other businesses to start it up. Give McD [former USAA Chairman General Robert F. McDermott] the credit. Mayor Cisneros, Red McCombs, and Ross Perot were key players too."

As the fateful year 1986 approached, the engines of the San Antonio economy were still purring and the bank providing spark plugs. Other Texas cities might suffer real estate nervous breakdowns, crippling recessions, even population losses. But San Antonio could only get bigger and better, the Frost powers calculated.

They were wrong. The rosy economic outlook there was more apparent than real. Warning signs were overlooked. San Antonio would enter 1986 with commercial construction and new hotels overbuilt, an overheated real estate market about to stall, business financing harder to get, and new industries that had promised to come breaking their promise. If the mid-Eighties had established beyond a doubt that Texas was not recession-proof, the late Eighties would establish it about San Antonio. An economic tornado worse than the one in 1983 was whirling toward the state. This time, the city would not be spared.

chapter 8

The Apocalypse: 1986

Minutes for the February 1986 Board meeting (with company stock trading at a lusty 21 1/8 and full recovery expected) reveal Frost management considering a sale/leaseback of the Frost Bank Tower. The April meeting discussed a sale of the Frost BankCard portfolio. The directors may have caught the whiff of another cyclone in the wind. Or perhaps they had learned that OPEC was about to drop an economic bomb on the West that would transform Texas banking again, this time permanently.

For Frost Bank, the 65-month Apocalypse ahead would see hundreds of relationship customers fall behind on loans to the brink of default, saddling it with devalued collateral. Again the Texas Oil Patch would be ravaged, causing an overleveraged energy industry to reel beneath the weight of excess capacity and inventory. The bell had rung for Round Two of the Eighties Energy Bust Battle; for this bank, that fateful decade would last not 10 years but 12.

Suddenly, during the first quarter of 1986, oil prices toppled from

$30 to $9.75 a barrel. Tired of shorting itself with curtailed production that benefited its OPEC competitors, Saudi Arabia, the oil-richest OPEC member, had taken the lead in flooding the world with cheap petroleum. This time, prices were cut by not one third but two. Texas exploration hit the canvas. According to a 1987 issue of *San Antonio Business* magazine, over a thousand rigs had operated in Texas at the height of the oil boom in 1981; by the third quarter of 1986, the figure was down to 226. Fortunes were lost, bankruptcies filed, and "Snowbirds" flew home. Investors shunned the state like a pariah. Texas lost 40,000 jobs. Houston lost population. Austin held emergency budget sessions at the Capitol. It was Texas's turn to burn while the nation fiddled.

This time, the flames spread to cities outside the Oil Patch. The state's honeymoon with long-term commercial real estate investment ended in acrimonious divorce. As oil prices plunged, Cullen/Frost perceived Houston real estate at risk and clamped down on construction loans there. But it did not clamp down on them as much in "nonenergy" cities like Dallas, Austin, and San Antonio. The company counted on its widespread geographical diversity. But all of Texas—including those nonenergy cities—was still in the energy business, whether it knew it or not. Banks may have forgotten that. And real estate developers may have forgotten how symbiotic was their industry's relationship with energy; how many investors were heavily leveraged in both fields; how they themselves could be submerged in a ripple effect should energy crash into the sea.

Admittedly, even Frost Bank fell victim to this contamination of error plaguing banking and real estate. Fortunately, however, its immune system was stronger than that of other banks, its exposure to the contamination milder. "Sure, a lot of the loans we'd made went bad," admits Dick Evans, the Frost Bank president and chief loan officer during the Apocalypse. "And I signed off on lots of 'em. But there's a saying: 'All loans are good when you make 'em. Some just turn bad later.' We'd been told we were running *out* of oil, and that Texas construction could only *grow*. There were cranes everywhere…office skyscrapers going up…new industrial parks…. Once you start building those things, you have to finish 'em. It takes two years just to slow down the expansion. Our mistakes we made for the right reasons; and the mistakes we didn't make we avoided for the right reasons…"

In other words, relationship banking prevailed; had it not, this history would be a tragedy. Unlike banks and thrifts still prey to rash and reckless practices, Cullen/Frost had learned from its 1983 mistakes and taken steps to correct them. Its 1985 loans for "raw" land and commercial development construction, for example, were only 11.4 percent of the portfolio.

But that was 11.4 percent too much. Frost Jr. admits, "We did lend on land that wasn't producing anything. Decades earlier, Uncle Joe had warned against loans on nonproducing assets, even gold. But I figured he'd have realized this situation was different. Property values kept rising. Sooner or later, there had to be development on those properties. Or so I thought. I was wrong."

Wisely, however, the bank stood by its traditional policy of refusing to lend with no liability on the borrower; it refused to even when relationship customers complained that "all the other banks," and the thrifts too, "were doing it." And the bad loans it did make, it made not to projects doomed to fail but to customers it knew and trusted involved in those projects. Even relationship banking and adherence to tradition could not avert serious problems. But they did, as Evans contends, narrow the field of losses. Luck was not a factor; deliberation, foresight, and the evaluation of character spelled the difference between survival and failure. As one holding company officer put it, "Picture a fleet of airplanes heading into turbulence. We were at the rear, so we could see what was happening to planes flying blind in front of us. That gave us time to make strategic decisions that prevented our crash."

The image is apt; as overaggressive banks and thrifts burst into flame, Cullen/Frost watched with mounting concern for itself and the community. Fittingly, one doomed S&L bought control of a funeral home. Another sank 90 percent of its deposits into short-term $100,000 CDs known as "hot" money and immolated itself with the heat. A few real estate wheeler-dealers, lured by the promise of "cheap" money, bought their own S&Ls and ran them into the ground all by themselves. With cruel irony, the regulatory easings allowed by the Carter and Reagan Administrations to ensure the survival of thrifts helped speed their demise. Nationally, over 1000 of them failed, leaving behind $400 billion in real estate to be liquidated. Only six of the top 100 Texas S&Ls survived.

Many banks—especially so-called "real estate banks"—fell prey to similar follies and required federal bailouts too. Or they were swallowed up by omnivorous megabanks. "Yes, we made bad loans," Dick Evans reprises, "but not as many as other financial institutions did. That's why we're still here and they're not."

Cullen/Frost's 1986 annual report announced a $6.5 million net loss, with a $41.1 million provision for possible loan losses, up by a whopping $18 million from the 1985 provision. Nonperforming assets had ballooned to $66.5 million. Net charge-offs for loans—$33.29 million—were 42 percent higher than in the previous year. It was also bad news that time deposit costs for Texas banks had risen compared to national averages, lessening the spread between earning assets and the cost of funds.

The news, however, was not all bad. The annual report pointed out that Cullen/Frost had not fared as badly in 1986 as its Texas peers had. Compared with them, it could boast "fewer problem loans; continued maintenance of high liquidity to deposits; larger resources in relation to problem loans; and net worth more than double non-performing asset levels." Times were tough, in other words, but they would have been even tougher with some other bank. The report also pointed to a healthy loan-to-deposit ratio of 55:45, which none of the eight other large Texas bank holding companies could match. In the words of a Frost senior vice-president, "This reassurance went back to Mr. Joe's emphasis on stressing how strong we were—not how big—and how safe customer deposits were. Our tellers could honestly assure nervous depositors that we were faring better than our competitors."

The bank also took pains to maintain its competitive presence in all its markets by soliciting new business—and to maintain its nurturing presence in those markets by supporting community projects. At this time, the useful concept of differentiating the "bad" Frost bank suffering loan woes from the "good" Frost bank healthy in every other respect was utilized. Attributed to Houston Cullen Bank President J. Gordon Muir Jr., the "good bank/bad bank" concept called for the comptroller to work up monthly figures detailing how the operation would be faring were it totally free of loan problems.

The figures were astonishing and uplifting. Taken with the idea, Frost Jr. spread its message to management at all the company's other banks. "Become too overly focused on your problems," went the message, "and you'll let the healthy aspects of your bank get sick too. Make sure you're confronting every problem a bank absolutely free of loan problems would be. That way, once your loan problems are solved, you'll still be a strong, healthy bank in every other respect."

"The idea worked," Robert S. McClane says today. "It worked so well, we even thought of creating a separate organization to spin off the assets of the 'bad' bank from those of the 'good' bank. We never took it that far, though…"

"Liquidity, liquidity, liquidity." Mr. Joe had repeated the lesson of the Great Depression like a mantra. In 1986, faced with mounting losses and the need for turnaround, or crisis, management, Cullen/Frost took seven significant steps to shore up capital:

(1) It sold its credit card business to a Delaware bank (forming an "agent" relationship with that bank's card company) at a $5.7 million profit;

(2) it liquidated its overfunded retirement plan, bought annuities from a Tennessee insurance company to fund employee pensions, and used the money saved to fund an ESOP (employee stock ownership plan) that increased company capital by $10.7 million while gifting workers with 800,000 unissued shares of Cullen/Frost stock;

(3) it restructured its medical and life insurance programs;

(4) it sold the appreciated municipal bonds it had bought in the early Eighties, netting a gain, and purchased "Zero Coupon" (internally compounded with no cash flow) municipal bonds it would sell, upon passage of pending tax legislation, at a bigger gain;

(5) it streamlined its work force by 10 percent and outsourced numerous functions, one of them its own bank data processing, to reduce costs;

(6) it drastically cut shareholder dividends for the second, third, and fourth quarters of the year; and

(7) it resolved to forge full-speed ahead into the area of indirect automobile financing, a dependable ancillary service.

The following year, 1987, to further shore up capital and reduce costs, two more steps were added to the multipoint plan: (1) The Tower/parking garage leaseback would be finalized for a $40 million sales price, and (2) the correspondent bank data processing center would be sold to Electronic Data Systems, or EDS, at a $6 million profit. These actions are discussed in the following chapter.

All nine strategies, some of which involved courageous risk, were not devised at one emergency confab; they were ground out in endless, grueling late-hour "Executive Committee" meetings tense with frayed nerves. But they dug up buried treasure. Robert S. McClane, holding company president at the time and architect of a good number of the strategies, estimates that all totalled they strengthened capital reserves by $100 million. Retired Chief Investment Officer George Mead, who masterminded the "Zero Coupon" maneuver, says, "We raised that capital at a time when we needed liquidity to survive and absolutely no Texas bank had any credit. Even harder times lay ahead. If we hadn't raised the capital, we likely wouldn't have made it through them."

With sweeping industry changes, 1986 proved a watershed year for Texas banking. In September, the State Legislature flung open the doors (1) for Texas banks to operate branches on a county-wide basis, and (2) for out-of-state banks to enter Texas through acquisitions.

To starving Texas banks, an influx of corpulently healthy ones spelled new capital sources: manna from heaven. To Cullen/Frost, branch banking meant added convenience for its customers, cost savings for the company, and the chance to unite all its banks (except the Galveston) under a single banner. As for the "barbarians at the gates," Frost Jr. privately stated that he did not like the idea of throwing open the state to outsiders. But in that respect, he found himself a minority of one: The other major bankers admitted that their institutions needed out-of-state capital to survive.

Already the year had seen mergers involving three of the state's largest banks: Texas Commerce Bancshares of Houston had merged with Chemical New York Corporation; RepublicBank Corporation of Dallas and InterFirst Corporation of Dallas had merged with each other. The world of Texas banking had changed unrecognizably in the three years since the (announced) First City merger. What choice had Cullen/Frost but to change with it?

chapter 9

Struggle, Survival, Recovery: 1987–1992

In 1987, the holding company fared better, though 1986 had been an easy act to follow. With earnings of $1.983 million, Cullen/Frost was the only major Texas bank holding company to report a profit for each of 1987's four quarters. From 1986's $41.1 million, loan loss provision declined to $27.9 million. Loan charge-offs, totaling $22.847 million, had been trimmed by a full third. The Cullen/Frost operation in Houston, the city hit hardest by oil busts, even showed a profit of $332,000 for the year.

"When the second oil bust hit in 1986," says Houston/Galveston Regional President Dave Beck, "our Houston Cullen bank was already in a healing mode. This time we were ready for it. We were well into dealing with our bad-loan problems by then."

But there was bad news too. Nonperforming assets, top-heavy with real estate loans, escalated by an alarming 41 percent—from $66.5 million in January to $93.7 million at year-end. As in 1986, knives were sharpened for cost-cutting: In February 1987, 43 more jobs were eliminated, bringing the 1986-1987 total to 277. Board minutes for that month's meeting record further discussion of a Frost Tower sale/lease-back. Minutes for the April meeting document the decision to eliminate all cash dividends for 12 months.

It is impossible to measure or describe the toll this crisis took on even the bank's sturdiest officers. They were involved in a grinding war of attrition, they were losing, and it seemed that this war, like an earlier war in Vietnam, would never end. Confidence was shaken, nerves frayed—people went without rest or sleep. The "team" had never been tested like this before. Frost Bank President Dick Evans, normally poised but beside himself over bad real estate loans, held staff meeting after staff meeting. His one-on-one Thursday meetings lasted longest. "Starting at one in the afternoon," he recalls, "I'd bring the loan officers who worked under me into my office one at a time. Rarely were we through before midnight, sometimes not before two a.m. Then I'd report to Tom [Frost Jr.] and finalize decisions we'd made."

Evans recalls dragging himself, fatigued to the point of tears, out of his office after a particularly grueling meeting on a night in 1987. He encountered Frost Jr. at the elevator. "Tom was heading out of town on one of his Houston or Dallas trips," he recalls. "In a tired voice, I asked, 'Tom, is there anything you need?' He said, 'Well…I always need you.'

"I've never forgotten that," Evans discloses. "It gave me the boost I needed to keep going at the low point of my life."

In June 1987, the Tower/parking garage leaseback was finalized, boosting capital reserves by another $40 million. The participating investment company was a partnership created by Steve Lee, a local real estate developer whose father, Quincy Lee, had been recruited as a bank employee by Mr. Joe in the Thirties. (San Antonio was a big town but a small world. Quincy Lee had gone on to become a local construction and real estate magnate in the postwar years, making a fortune in home building. He served on the Frost Bank Board from 1967—and on the Cullen/Frost Board from 1977—until his death in 1997. Quincy was also a chairman of the Frost Bank Audit Committee, on which he served from 1983 until 1994, when he retired from it for health reasons.)

The 1987 leaseback agreement stipulated that the bank retain the option to buy back the Tower when it wished to. Still, "it was painful," Steve Lee recalls. "The negotiations were difficult, complicated…There were exhausting late-night meetings. I know how it must've hurt. But it was something Frost Bank had to do, and it turned out well for everyone."

Another 1987 divestiture to raise capital involved the sale of the correspondent bank data processing center to EDS, or Electronic Data Systems. For 20 years, the data processing center had faithfully performed basic data-managing services for several dozen correspondent banks as well as for Frost. Finally, however, it had become an albatross. "It was too resource-intensive," Robert S. McClane remembers. "Every time we had to change a system at our bank, we had to sell all those other banks on the change. We were taking more care of our correspondent banks than ourselves. We made another nice profit on the sale." Henceforth, major processing of Frost time accounts would be performed on the premises through a facility management system owned by the company ALTEL.

The bank found itself in a punishing race in 1987. As its fallout from bad loans accumulated, it had to shore up reserves ever faster.

It was a time when more and more bankers were discovering that trusts were not just solid assets in the bank but a way for the bank to make money. By June 30, 1987, Frost Bank's Common Stock Fund boasted an average annual return of 31 percent, which put it in the top 10 percent of all equity managers nationwide. With its steadily growing trust management businesses (company farm and ranch managers supervised 2.6 million total surface areas in 18 states and Canada), which commanded increased fees, Cullen/Frost would see its trust assets exceed $6.2 billion by year-end 1987.

Strategically, on October 1, 1987, all Frost investment services, including the four-year-old Discount Brokerage, were consolidated under the Trust Department. Explained Richard Kardys, executive trust officer since 1980, "We wanted to make sure staff members weren't competing for customers. We wanted a unified investment approach. We felt that the sum of the individual parts could be greater functioning as part of a whole than separately."

✦ ✦ ✦

Fast as the bank was changing, Texas was changing faster, showing the world a new economic face. Diversification had proved the silver lining in the cloud of energy woes.

By 1987, according to a Cullen/Frost annual report, more Texans were working in service industries than in the three goods-producing categories—manufacturing, oil and gas, and construction—combined. Unbelievably, Texas would be less dependent by 1989 than the nation as a whole on goods-producing sources of employment. Petroleum, agriculture, and real estate would actually contribute less to Texas wealth than service industries (including health care), retailing, computer manufacturing, high tech, and biosciences. For Texas banks, it was going to be a whole new ball game; for Cullen/Frost, only the rules, relationship banking rules, would remain the same.

But the game started slowly. It was a cautiously profitable reconstructive era of slowly but surely building up Cullen/Frost reserves and shoring up Cullen/Frost capital: a steady if laborious trek up the comeback trail. It was also a time of wisely focusing on the customer as never before to enhance franchise value for the long haul regardless of how hard times might seem for the short one.

Customer convenience became more compelling a concern than ever. Over 1988-1989, with branch banking finally legal, all the holding company's San Antonio banks, including the Kelly Air Force Base facility, were consolidated into a single Frost Bank. Also, the Letter to Shareholders for 1989 announced the acquistion of "five smaller banks in the San Antonio area." Three of them—Westpoint, University, and Summit—were failed suburban banks, purchased from the FDIC. Convenient new locations for the Frost customer were thereby created.

The net result was an efficient one-bank, 10-office branching system so widely dispersed throughout the area as to give Frost Bank customers more convenience than they had ever enjoyed. As a result, Frost soon boasted a 26 percent market share of all Bexar County deposits. Said a confident Dick Evans to the press, "No more layoffs among our eleven hundred San Antonio workers are expected. As we continue to expand, we'll use existing staff at our new locations."

Another example of the push for Frost customer convenience was the major contract, signed in April 1988, between the bank and the state's largest grocery store chain, H-E-B. This contract, which would be renewed in January 1994 and again in March 1998, ensured that Frost Bank customers could use the ATMs in all H-E-B supermarkets free of charge. Needless to say, the move was smiled upon by Frost account holders, who, like most people, had grown annoyed at having to pay a fee for the convenience of using ATMs at locations other than their bank itself. And the contract– which is expected to be renewed a third time, in the year 2003—benefited H-E-B as well; it gave customers one more reason to shop in H-E-B stores.

In 1988, for the second consecutive year, Cullen/Frost had reported modest profits during all four quarters. Gains for that year totaled $2.4 million: a respectable figure for which grateful shareholders gave thanks and praise. Nonperforming assets had risen by just $4.5 million, down from an alarming $27.2 million growth in 1987. Company stock value continued to climb, and to fuel rumors of outside interest and impending takeover—rumors nobody at the bank believed. In the air was the sweet scent of optimism, fresh as a spray of cologne.

For all its steady progress, however, the bank was not lulled into the false confidence of its rebound after the 1983 debacle. Nonperforming assets, most of them in real estate, had climbed to an alarming $98.2 million and continued to hang over the bank's head like a Sword of Damocles. Says Tom Frost Jr., "We were the healthiest of the big Texas holding companies at the time, because we were the only one that wasn't broke. But we were the weakest if you included those who'd just come into the market, like Chemical Bank and North Carolina National."

That was a paradox: The numbers had painted a prettier picture than the real one. Despite the fleet's overall profit, three of its ships—Parkdale, Frost Bank North Austin, and the Dallas Citizens National—were torpedoed by 1988 losses, with Frost Bank North Austin's $5.8 million the highest. The energy cyclone had rocked Corpus Christi since 1986; the real estate cyclone had rocked Austin in 1987, Dallas in 1988.

Who was next? Could it be San Antonio, the flagship city where Frost Bank profits were twice those of the company's other profitable banks combined? Yes, it could. Accordingly, prudence and foresight prompted the bank to abandon its expensive dream of a Two Frost Tower. In its place, plans were announced for a $2 million "Greenbelt"—a tree-lined park to fill the vacant square block north of the existing Tower—and for the landscaping of two adjacent parking lots. Plans called for a 50-foot-wide pedestrian walkway, bright with Texas wildflowers.

The Greenbelt development affirmed Frost Bank's financial support for San Antonio's "Tri-Party" project—an ambitious downtown renovation-and-beautification effort that focused on bustling Houston Street. As a Downtown Merchants and Property Owners Association executive committee member, Frost Jr. had helped launch the project, which allied three key "parties": the Association, the city transit company, and the city itself. Remarkably, bond funding was raised via a taxing authority through which the downtown owners literally taxed themselves for the project. Even more remarkably, however, the Greenbelt was constructed with Frost money on Frost property as a private contribution to the project, independent of Tri-Party tax funding.

A stoic Tom Frost Jr. told the press, "Time has eliminated the need for a Two Frost Tower. Factors have intervened—the downturn in local real estate, the rise in interest rates, an economy heading south. And really, with branch banking, the need for an additional building and that much downtown space is gone." A fond dream was dead; as always, the bank adapted to harsh reality.

A "poison pill" is a strategic defensive employed by a target company to make its stock less attractive to acquirers and predators. In the Eighties, poison pills were commonly swallowed to provide shareholders protection against undesired takeovers. On July 27, 1989, a headline in the *San Antonio Express-News* blared CULLEN/FROST ADOPTS "POISON PILL."

The pill Cullen/Frost adopted was a shareholder rights protection plan—declaring a dividend of one "right" for each outstanding share of common stock—that would make a hostile takeover too expensive. Threatened by a takeover not Board-approved, stockholders would have "rights" to purchase enough additional shares to stop the takeover cold. (Should the Board agree to the takeover, however, rights would not come into play.)

Again the grapevine was abuzz with takeover rumors. Company spokespersons denied that the poison pill had been adopted to repel any specific advance. "Most major corporations have done this," they assured reporters, "and very few have had to use it." Nevertheless, company officers disagree to this day as to whether there ever was "a specific advance." Some say Yes, others No, and Tom Frost Jr. puts it like this: "We had people come in and tell us 'Anytime you'd like to talk about selling your bank, talk to us.' I told them that time would never come."

Nineteen-eighty-nine found the corporation's figurative head "bloody but unbowed." Earnings were slightly up for the third consecutive year. In the decade's twilight, trust assets stood at $8 billion, having mushroomed from $564.154 million in 1979. Miraculously, though the Eighties had seen it write off an astronomic $232 million in bad loans, Cullen/Frost was going to come out of the horrendous decade with the same amount of capital it had going in.

Over 1988-1989, the holding company had both expanded and consolidated, opening five new locations, as mentioned, in the San Antonio area but merging its Austin and Corpus Christi offices into Frost National Bank and its three Houston banks into Cullen Bank. Now Cullen/Frost comprised four banks—one each in San Antonio, Dallas, Houston, and Galveston—with a total of 21 offices. "Not only does this [reorganization] enhance customer convenience," explained the company's 1989 Letter to Shareholders, "but it brings significant cost savings."

Actually, the reorganization was a decisive step in the holding company's march to a goal it soon would realize: the consolidation of all its banks except Galveston's USNB under the Frost Bank banner. Today a clear and logical progression can be traced in the Frost journey from private bank to national bank to multi-bank holding company to single bank (outside of Galveston) with multiple branches. That progression is one more example of the bank's traditional flexibility—its ability to move in the direction required by its situation, its environment, its industry, and the era.

Meanwhile, the frantic race between problem-loan loss and recapitalization wore on. Wary of lending to ailing Texas businesses, the bank had watched its loans decline by $195 million in 1989 alone. For three consecutive years, it had reported minimal profits for every quarter and stored everything else into reserves. But how long could that continue? By 1990, its well of "hidden" reserves had run dry while its load of real estate baggage had grown heavier. "I had to wonder," Frost Jr. allows, "how much longer this could last. But I never felt we wouldn't make it. Never."

All the same, time was a factor, the clock speeding. Rising expenses incurred from carrying that much repossessed real estate had consumed $8.1 million in reserves. It became necessary to create a separate reserve to protect against declines in the value of such real estate. The properties were like excess cargo on an airplane, causing a loss of altitude by the hour. Unless the cargo was jettisoned, piece by piece and soon, the plane would crash. It might have crashed already had Cullen/Frost not been late flying into the storm.

By 1990, Tom Frost Jr. had relieved Frost Bank management of the responsibility for dealing with lingering problem assets. Now he looked for help from within the holding company. The bank had liquidity, but the cost of administering the real estate was enormous—it averaged 25 percent of the real estate's asset value every year. Frost needed to convert all that foreclosed real estate into earning assets posthaste.

The chairman had perceived that other banks faced with the dilemma always made a fatal mistake: They told a bank loan officer, "You're now a real estate expert!" and sent him off to war against the foreclosed-property nemesis. The loan officer never returned. Tom Frost Jr. would not make that mistake. He needed a nonbanker, a real estate specialist, to send off to war. And serendipitously, the holding company had one, having hired him in January 1989 to create a department that could study the formidable problem.

Frost Jr. sent for him. Stan McCormick was a Texan who had practiced law in Washington, D.C. before going into commercial real estate. He had spent a year working for the holding company president, Robert S. McClane. He would spend the next two and a half years working for the chairman, Tom Frost Jr.

McCormick's two loves were law and real estate. Although he had earned his law degree from the UT Law School, he had also taken every real estate course available at The University of Texas at Austin Business School. But he learned commercial real estate "out on the street," in his words, "in the neighborhoods: the only place you can learn it. You certainly can't learn it in a book." A genial red-haired man, McCormick not only knew how to negotiate a sale of foreclosed real estate and close it fast but also had a network in mind for unloading the Cullen/Frost baggage.

"I understood investors and developers and the games they play to take advantage of a bank," says the specialist, whose current position is corporate counsel and who in 1999 would become secretary to the Cullen/Frost Board. Still, he had to think twice about taking the job. He knew Cullen/Frost was in trouble, with the same problems that had sunk its strongest competitors, and that people at the bank were afraid. "I was afraid too," he confesses. "I had a reputation to protect. I didn't want it on my résumé that I'd worked for a company that failed. I could see myself on a ship with water up to the third deck.

"Yet the captain didn't seem afraid," he adds. "So I came aboard."

Right away, "the captain" schooled the attorney in traditional Frost philosophy with an object lesson in Frost integrity. McCormick recalls selling a foreclosed warehouse near the San Antonio International Airport in 1990. An interested buyer's offer had been accepted with a handshake. Then another interested buyer made a higher offer.

"Legally, we don't have an obligation to the first buyer," McCormick advised the banker.

Frost Jr. leaned back and thought about it. "Stan," he said, "I understand that. But is this how one human being should treat another?"

After a pause, McCormick said, "No, sir. It's not."

"Go with the first buyer. He negotiated in good faith. And don't use our second offer as leverage to up the price."

Stan McCormick knew he had found a leader he could follow into battle.

Back to 1989 for a recap of the decade. To have survived the Eighties was cause for any Texas bank to rejoice. For the time being, at least, Frost had repulsed the fiercest attacks in its history while adding trophies to its shelf. Since 1979, Cullen/Frost had increased shareholder equity by 73 percent, maintained its customer base, doubled its assets, tripled its number of offices, kept intact its cadre of officers and key employees, and enjoyed unflagging support from its Board.

It had also enjoyed another decade of futuristic high-tech innovation. In the Eighties, Automated Teller Machines (ATMs) with proliferating service capabilities had become as ubiquitous as McDonald's restaurants; with their Automated Teller Cards, they were the realization of a dream: around-the-clock banking. Meanwhile, on-line personal computers (PCs), deployed throughout the company, eliminated individual use of ponderous mainframe computers, with their need for programmer aid, and saved thousands of work hours.

The Local Area Network (LAN) linked those company PCs, eliminating the need for modems while facilitating communication with the bank and each other. Wire transfers expedited the traffic of money and information between banks, between cities, even up to the Fed itself. A new system called Branch Banker provided employees in the new accounts area with instant knowledge of what other services and accounts new customers had—or did not have but might need—without the tedium of their filling out forms.

Says Dick Evans, "We stayed current with the forefront of technology no matter what else was happening. We insisted on controlling that part of our lives, since it increased market share. That was a key decision we made in the Eighties."

It had also been a decade of high tech for San Antonio, which, like all of Texas, was diversifying economically. By 1990, that $100 million 1500-acre Texas Research Park had taken shape, with a University of

Texas Institute of Biotechnology about to grace its grounds. Broad-based support for research and development had led to Ph.D. programs in the biosciences and engineering at The University of Texas at San Antonio (UTSA). High-tech VLSI joined Sony as the city's second major microchip company, building a $200 million semiconductor plant that would hire 1000 employees. Japanese investment followed when Colin Electronics announced plans to produce blood pressure-monitoring equipment in San Antonio.

Earlier in the decade, Frost Bank had teamed up with the National Bank of Commerce and Alamo National Bank to "bankroll" a $100,000 feasibility study for a $200 million Rivercenter retail complex, anchored by a 1000-room Marriott Rivercenter Hotel that could host major conventions without conventioneers ever setting foot outside it. By 1989, widely touted as the best downtown mall in the country, Rivercenter (which had opened the previous year) was drawing record crowds. The feasibility study—conducted by the Rouse Company, which had built the city's first shopping mall, North Star, 30 years earlier—was one more example of San Antonio's growing willingness to take the bull by the horns and make things happen for itself.

The second wave of firms relocating to the Alamo City, begun in the mid-Eighties, had yet to crest by 1989. Besides the high-tech firms mentioned above, they had names like Bausch & Lomb, Sears Teleservice Center, Signtech, Alcoa/Fujikura (Pep Industries), and VNU Operations (Birch Research). Two Wal-Marts, a Sam's Wholesale Club, and the wildly popular Sea World opened in 1988. (To flash forward, a Fiesta Texas theme park, seasonally employing 2000 workers, would open in 1992 and the controversial $160 million Alamodome in 1993.) It should be noted that from 1987 to 1989, as Mayor Cisneros and the EDF recruited over 4000 new jobs for San Antonio, the EDF chairman was Cullen/Frost President Robert S. McClane.

Tourism became an annual $1.4 billion bonanza as hotel occupancy rates surpassed 80 percent. The Medical Center now employed

18,000 workers. Trade volume between San Antonio and Mexico passed the $55 million mark and was projected to double before the year 2000. As the post-Cisneros era dawned, the town where over 70 percent of Cullen/Frost assets were concentrated appeared economically healthy as the proverbial mule.

The appearance was a little deceiving. There was a bigger picture, not so bright or optimistic. Since 1986, for all its exciting new companies, economic diversification, mushrooming growth, and galvanizing leadership, San Antonio had been falling into an economic swoon from overbuilding and a drooping real estate industry. Soon its mettle would be tested, as had that of Houston, Austin, and Dallas. And once more, as the decade ground to a close, the condition of the bank and that of the city mirrored one another. Even in its darkest hours, however, the bank would continue to support San Antonio community endeavors, just as Cullen/Frost supported them in other company cities. But more so. Wherever it expanded, this bank's heart would belong to San Antonio, its hometown. Besides, it was good business: Frost needed to maintain the profile of its "good" bank, which enjoyed genuine success, even as it struggled with the problems of its "bad" bank, staggering beneath the onerous burden of bad loans and repossessed real estate.

The Nineties began not with a bang but a whimper. For Cullen/Frost, the Eighties might have been over, but its headaches were not. Nineteen-ninety was a ruinous year, with net losses of $8.22 million, sabotaging a winning streak of 15 consecutive profitable quarters.

The saboteur was a staggering but unavoidable loan-loss addition to reserves during a disastrous third quarter, hiking them up to $45.6 million: an all-time high. Most alarming was the fact that except for a Dallas bank mired in commercial-real-estate-loan quicksand, the heaviest losses were reported in San Antonio, where the company superstar took a $4.146 million red-ink bath after reporting a profit for every year of the Eighties. As the last Cullen/Frost market to feel the doldrums of the Texas downturn, San Antonio would be the last to shake them off.

What had happened? A 15-year building binge had ground to a halt, leaving the city in a state of dazed denial. *The Wall Street Journal* reported 1990 commercial San Antonio real estate vacancies at 31 percent, the highest in Texas. "Nobody thought it would happen to San Antonio," said Robert Rieke, a vice-president in the Dallas investment banking firm Rauscher Pierce Refsnes. "But it did."

The *San Antonio Express-News* explained it this way: A big under-developed town had been discovered by opportunistic out-of-town developers with unlimited resources from S&Ls, banks, and tax-sheltered limited partnerships. Money (and civic concern) being no object, major new buildings had risen, and others been renovated, with zero regard for economizing. Land prices tripled, quadrupled—an acre that had sold for $8000 in 1980 cost $30,000 by 1984. Nobody bought it. Spurred by newly available mortgage-backed bonds, apartments went up twice as fast as needed, and half of them remained vacant. Now the party was over and the piper had to be paid. As though shouldering the blame for the city's woes, Tom Frost Jr. told the press, "My major mistake of omission was not foreseeing that sooner or later, San Antonio real estate would be impacted by the drop in oil prices."

That oversight seems inconceivable: As of 1987, according to *San Antonio Business* magazine, no fewer than 500 San Antonio firms were involved in some way with the energy industry. "I made the same mistake in Dallas," the banker adds today. "Neither was a heavy energy town, really, though they had energy firms. I thought both cities might escape. San Antonio had carried our whole operation during the Eighties. Had it gotten hit then, we wouldn't be here now."

Keener foresight had been exercised in Houston, where the twice-recapitalized Cullen Bank reported $6.89 million in 1990 positive earnings. Houston, the state's first casualty of the energy crash and its slowest to heal, now led its recovery with a 2.92 percent 1990 job growth. Meanwhile, Dallas continued to be punished for the sin of speculative real estate lending with a slowdown in construction, finance, and defense on *top* of real estate. The ripple effect. Austin too lagged behind, with massive construction job losses and the sharpest employment tail-off among Texas cities, after having created new jobs faster than any other. Still, Cullen/Frost's little North Austin (Chase) bank eked out 1990 profits of $20,000 after four straight years in the red.

The Corpus Christi and Galveston operations enjoyed modest profits too. Corpus Christi's Parkdale bank had rebounded after two straight (and five out of seven) losing years. Says Corpus Christi Regional President Mike Carrell, "What allowed us to survive the bottom dropping out of the energy market in an Oil Patch town was our refineries on the ship channel. As oil prices fell, those refineries got cheaper raw materials for their hydrocarbon plants. This town didn't lose one refinery. Refineries closed in other towns and moved here. Our refineries more than made up for the thousands of jobs we lost in oil and gas." The Coastal Bend area even saw expansion. Board minutes for the corporation's April 1990 meeting record a decision, finalized in 1991, to absorb the region's Portland State Bank. This little bank had suffered in the Eighties, borrowed heavily from Cullen/Frost, suffered even more, and offered itself to the holding company as repayment of the loan. In the Nineties, newly secure as a Frost branch, it would fare better.

The Galveston market seemed disaster-proof. Its bank had never rebounded, because it had never slumped. Solid old USNB, acquired in the Kempner merger, had recorded stable profits every year of the Eighties; with earnings of $2.673 million, 1990 was its best year yet. Since Galveston had not enjoyed an energy boom, it had not suffered an energy bust; despite its proximity to Houston, it did not have an oil-and-gas economy or want one. Says USNB President F. A. "Andy" Odom, "We in Galveston never had the *opportunity* to make the mistakes Houston did. We were a community bank in every respect, with involvement ranging from City Hall to school boards to Galveston College."

Odom adds that somewhere around 1990, the USNB attained banking's Holy Grail: Its noninterest income exceeded its overhead; all net interest income from lending money went straight to the bottom line: profit. "That's why in 1997," Odom adds, "the American Bankers Association *Banking Journal* named us the seventh most profitable bank in the country with assets of between a hundred million and a billion dollars. It doesn't hurt, thanks to Shrub Kempner's genius for picking stocks, that we have the biggest trust department in Galveston, either."

Nineteen-ninety was a year of Cullen/Frost turnaround, not growth, management. Still, there was growth. Over 1989-1990, three banks were acquired from the Kerrville-based Schreiner Bancshares, Inc. holding company: the First National Bank of Boerne, the (nearby) Fair Oaks National Bank, and the First National Bank of Fredericksburg. Two of the banks would be kept as part of the Frost Bank system; the Fredericksburg bank, however, which opened as a Frost branch early in 1990 with assets of $22 million and deposits of $21 million, would be sold to Fort Worth-based Team Bank.

There was expansion within Frost Bank as well. In 1990, Patrick Frost, Tom Frost Jr.'s youngest son, became the first head of the newly created Retail Division. In banking parlance, "retail" is a blanket term that covers individual and small-business accounts as distinct from large commercial ones. The new division was created partially as a response to the 1986 authorization of branch banking in Texas, one result of which was that the corporation's individually chartered banks could now be consolidated as Frost branches.

"Because we had a very decentralized operation," says Patrick Frost, the current Frost president, "we wanted to make sure all our branches were delivering retail services uniformly, using the same procedures.

The emphasis is different now, of course. We've learned how to do branch banking, so we try for a community retail focus in every region, allowing every bank to be a little different." As of 1998, under the helmsmanship of Executive Vice-President Kenneth A. Trapp, the Retail Division remained an important part of the company's overall operation. Many small businesses looking for loans head straight to the branch banks, or "financial centers," because of the convenience factor. The San Antonio and Corpus Christi retail operations are preeminent.

✦ ✦ ✦

So much for 1990 growth and expansion. The company's crisis management team had its hands full. The year had been Cullen/Frost's worst since 1986. Again its banks were falling behind in the race, taking two steps forward and three back. Conceivably, some law of diminishing returns held that the longer the race continued, the smaller were the company's chances of winning. By 1990, for all the good its "good" bank was doing, Cullen/Frost's survival may have hinged upon liquidating its vast acreage of foreclosed real estate.

It seemed an impossible task. But a determined Stan McCormick and Frost Jr. rolled up their sleeves and tackled it in methodical fashion. "Tom gave me free rein and a wonderfully competent and professional support staff," the attorney recalls. "First we had to *find* all that repossessed real estate. Then we had to get a file started on each parcel. Soon there were hundreds of files—forty million dollars worth of foreclosures—staring us in the face."

From early 1990 until well into 1992, the banker and the lawyer launched a frontal assault upon that stack of files, flying to Austin, Corpus Christi, Houston, and Dallas, calling on Cullen/Frost CEOs and real estate loan officers. In each city, and San Antonio too, they encountered executives in denial who could not bear to sell devalued real estate appraised at, say, $1 million for half that sum but wanted to hang on to it, as though it were a slumping stock, until the "market rallied."

McCormick admits that by himself he could not have made those executives see the light. He remembers Frost Jr.'s approach to them as being polite but firm. "Gentlemen," the banker would begin, "this property is not worth what you think. If we hold onto it to get that price, we aren't going to succeed. We have to sell it at the appropriate market price on a given day. The market is stronger than any of us."

In each instance, the reluctant officers relented and relinquished the properties. McCormick then undertook the grim task of selling them off, piece by piece. Some days, some entire weeks, he did not sell any. "I went into Tom's office one Monday morning," he recalls, "and he asked, 'How'd we do last week?' I told him we'd sold one lot—in Corpus Christi—for five thousand dollars. He got real quiet. He leaned back, gazed up at the ceiling, and said, 'Stan, that's one less lot we'll have to sell. Good job.'

"Other bosses," McCormick adds, "would have thrown an ashtray at me. I was so motivated, I marched out of there and worked past midnight."

After that, the tide began to turn. Slowly but surely, the repossessed properties began to sell. Every month, McCormick's stack of files grew shorter. The bank pulled dead even in the race. Then the bank pulled ahead.

But even then, victory was not assured: 1991 recorded $13.237 million in new net loan charge-offs. The race wore on. Even on its toughest laps, McCormick remembers, the banker's demeanor remained cheerful. Frost Jr. was a man named for the Colonel, McCormick stresses, with everything he had worked for all his life—plus 120 years of family tradition—in jeopardy. His friends in other banks had lost everything, and now their banks had strange non-Texas-sounding names. The stock of his own bank was down to $5 a share. How could he not show fear?

"Grace under pressure," the attorney concludes. "He must've been scared. But he had to hide it. It wasn't just the Frost tradition. He's got some kind of internal compass that points due north. It's how he's wired together…"

By the autumn of 1991, survival seemed probable. McCormick's stack had been whittled down to a few files. Loan quality was improving with every quarter. But nobody was popping champagne corks. By year-end, nonperforming assets had dropped by $21 million, to just $10 million. After two straight years of $28 million-plus loan charge-offs, the total declined by more than half. Losses on OREO (other real estate owned) sales had plummeted from $519,000 to zero, and the company netted a $205,000 profit that seemed like $205 million.

Blessedly, though still hurting, the San Antonio Frost Bank rebounded from its devastating 1990 losses with an $869,000 profit for the year. The local picture had brightened. Henry Cisneros was gone, but those firms he had courted kept coming, and the bank, along with public organizations and other private companies, continued to welcome them. In 1990 alone, West Telemarketing Outbound and Sony Semiconductor Company of America delivered a total of 5000 new jobs. In 1991, diverse firms like Citicorp, QVC Network, Foxmeyer, Teleservice Resources, Humana Corp., and AA Direct Marketing Corp. created 7000 more jobs. The city, like the bank, was on a comeback.

How had this old bank survived? One means was through noninterest income in the form of fees—deposit accounts, cash management and investment services, trust operations—that sustained liquidity and the solid assets requisite for survival. Additionally, survival was a cornerstone of this bank's history, an inheritance from its founder, himself a born survivor; this bank had a dominant survival gene. But the deciding factors, as always, had been its philosophy, traditions, and reliance on common values and trusting relationships already in place. In two words—relationship banking.

Robert T. Huthnance, then president of the Dallas bank, remembers, "Only one problem loan surprised us from a *character* standpoint.

It was to a Dallas real estate developer. He was well thought of in the community, and we thought well of him too. But he looked us square in the eye and said, 'Gentlemen, I'm gonna stiff you. Here's how I can beat you out of this loan. So negotiate. Let me off the hook.'

"We did, too," Huthnance continues. "We had to release his guarantee, because he had no liquidity. What hurt most was, we'd trusted him. Everybody else we had a relationship with did everything they could to pay us." The exception had proved the rule.

Another ally in the victory had been the Frost tradition of shifting from growth to turnaround management in the hour of crisis without the upheaval of turnover. Frost stuck with the people who had gotten it there. As Mr. Joe had put it, "We make our decisions together, we confront our problems together, we solve them together." Loyalty was a key ingredient in a survival recipe that did not include scapegoating, revolving doors, pointing fingers, rolling heads, or new brooms sweeping clean. Few other Texas banks could say that. New assignments had gone to existing officers. The closest person to an "outsider" or newcomer—Stan McCormick, the real estate specialist—had been assigned to Frost Bank from its holding company.

Nor had there been heroes—not McCormick, not even Frost Jr. It had been a team effort: The team that had made the mistakes was the team that corrected them. And huge team mistakes had been made. Some—like overaggressive lending on energy and real estate, a failure to perceive how cyclical were those industries, and the assumption that the tidal wave of energy woe would not engulf non-energy-dependent cities—were obvious. Others were subtler, internal, organizational.

As the worst of those, the bank cites (1) too much decentralization without closely supervised loan review; (2) lack of a "trust and inspect" and a "risk assessment" process to detect problems and confront them early on; (3) lack of a "central information system" to keep track of what loans each officer made, what interest rates they carried, what past-dues were outstanding; and (4) lack of a "credit administration" to oversee the entire loan picture and pinpoint top-heavy product or geographic concentrations.

By 1993, the bank had corrected those four mistakes. "Still," Tom Frost Jr. says, "all the assessment systems in the world are no good if you're not basing your decisions on sound values and a consistent philosophy. To the extent that we strayed from that, we got into trouble." And what about greed, the Eighties' cardinal sin? "Yes, we fell into some of that," the banker admits. "As did other banks. There was so much money out there. But ours was not an overwhelming or consuming greed. More often than not, our values overcame our greed.

"Besides," he adds with a thoughtful grin, "I'm not sure that if we'd been *totally* cautious and just sat back during the Boom, we'd have come out of that, either. Standing pat would've cost us market share. That was a mistake we'd made when I first came to work at the bank and the Depression scare was fresh in everyone's memory. The good thing about mistakes is, you learn from them. We'll do better during the next disaster—and there will be one—because we won't make the same mistakes.

"We learned a lot from the ordeal," he concludes. "*I* learned a lot. I'd always known this was a special bank to work in, but never really understood why. Now I do."

By mid-1992, the Apocalypse, as bankers called it, was history. During the previous 10 years, Texas banks had bitten the dust at an even faster clip than the Great Depression had triggered. Over 500 of them failed: more than one-third of all failures nationally. Of the state's 10 largest financial institutions, only Cullen/Frost had not failed or required FDIC assistance or been absorbed by a larger concern.

The bank was still one of the 10 largest in the state. But now, with Texas banking reconstituted and out-of-state leviathans like North Carolina National (NCNB) and Bank One in the picture, that meant something altogether different. Frost no longer envisioned itself as a big bank but as a big community bank, with a new mission stated in its annual report for 1992: "We will position ourselves between the mega-banks and the community bankers, offering a more personal, responsive service than the larger organizations and a broader range of products and services than the smaller banks." That new mission was a way of recapturing, if on a different scale, the traditional position it had cherished for so many decades. As 1993 dawned, comfortable in a niche old and new to it, Frost Bank was at peace with itself and the world again.

chapter 10

A New Mission: 1993-1996

On February 12, 1993, by acquiring the Austin and San Antonio offices of its old friend First City (now New First City) Bancorporation of Texas, Cullen/Frost was again Number One in assets among independent Texas-based banking firms. And Frost National was again Number One in Alamo City deposits, having earlier lost top market share to NCNB Texas (later NationsBank).

With the failure of First City and its sale by the FDIC, the corporation stood alone as the sole Top-10 Texas bank holding company to have survived the Eighties intact. Its 1992 net income, $24.1 million, was its highest since 1982; in 1993 the figure would almost double, to $47.2 million. Its $206 million in 1992 equity capital was the most in the corporation's history. Noninterest income hit $61.8 million, one-third of it from trust fees. Reserves from lingering problem loans had been cut from 1991's $42 million to $32 million, nonperforming assets cut in half, and sales of foreclosed assets were up 42 percent.

By year-end 1993, the bank's renewed confidence was palpable. A 10 percent stock dividend had been paid for the year's first quarter, and cash dividends were resumed during the fourth quarter. The extraordinary recovery had put Frost Bank back on the growth track and made the New First City gambit possible.

This acquisition, which meant another San Antonio office downtown (at 711 Navarro), cost the bank $38 million: its largest expenditure up to that point. But it also meant 23 branches now in two of the state's highest job-growth markets and $496 million in total corporate assets. Deposit-wise, the bank became not just Number One in San Antonio but Number Six in Austin as well.

The history of First City, or New First City, was a textbook study in banking misfortune. As of 1980, First City Bancorporation had been *the* energy lender in Houston. But it never recovered from the energy disaster of 1983. After its merger with Cullen/Frost fell through in 1985, its troubles deepened with the second energy cataclysm in 1986, during which it managed to lose $406.1 million. In 1987, with somehow greater losses anticipated, the FDIC announced it would help former Chicago banker A. Robert Abboud acquire First City, as a "rescue," by contributing $970 million to its recapitalization.

But ultimately, the rescue failed. By 1992, First City was at the end of its rope. The FDIC stepped in again, this time as auctioneer, selling the corporation's 20 banks to 12 bidders, one of whom was Frost National, for a total of just $434 million.

Bidding on First City banks was the first step in Cullen/Frost's master plan for renewed expansion. Healthy again, ready to climb back into the ring, the corporation was already an established presence in the Houston/Galveston market, with downtown banks and sizable trust assets. But it operated just a medium-sized bank in downtown Dallas, a small suburban bank in Austin, and a medium-sized bank in Corpus Christi that was not downtown either. It lacked the resources for a power play in Big D. That left Austin and Corpus Christi.

"It made sense for us to operate from Austin *south*ward," says Robert T. Huthnance, who moved from Cullen/Frost Dallas (formerly Citizens National) to become president of First City Austin as soon as the deal closed. "Our Dallas bank was doing all right again, but gearing up for a power play there would have cost too much. In Austin, we could have the big downtown bank we wanted and a ready-made trust department; Austin was the center of trust activity for the whole state." Not that the First City acquisition came cheap. Besides the $38 million auction pricetag, the twice-ravaged bank would need to be fully recapitalized. Huthnance discloses that First City Austin had seen its commercial loan volume dwindle to just $25 million. (He proudly adds that by June 1998, five years later, it would be 10 times that amount, with half a billion dollars in trust assets.)

"Who would've thought we'd end up paying $38 million for *First City*?" asks Frost Bank President Patrick Frost today. "My dad took a big gamble there. But it sure paid off. If he hadn't taken the chance, we wouldn't have that star shining in our galaxy."

With a south-from-Austin direction of renewed growth established, the corporation was faced with the delicate question of what to do with its lone Dallas operation. From 1988 through 1991, its troubled Cullen/Frost Dallas bank had posted a negative net income of over $18 million; now, though, with its horrific real estate messes cleaned up, it was posting profits again. The trouble was, it had no future in the master plan. Too much management and capital would be needed to make it fly competitively in the upper echelons of Dallas finance, where banks competed for dollars and market share in a new dimension. It had to be let go.

With Huthnance dispatched to First City Austin, the corporation replaced him at the Dallas bank with Frost Bank Senior Executive Vice-President and loan specialist R. E. ("Buster") Fawcett Jr. Says Fawcett, who had seen troubleshooting duty at the North Austin Bank and the Coastal Bend area's Portland State, "At that time, we didn't know what we were gonna do with Cullen/Frost Dallas. I sort of baby-sat it a few months, as president, while living in a Dallas hotel."

What transpired that summer, as the bank again cast eyes on the Coastal Bend, was both a study in serendipity and a test of its traditional flexibility. As the result of a long-distance cellular phone call to Tom Frost Jr. (driving in his automobile to Austin) from Texas Commerce Bank CEO Marc Shapiro at TCB headquarters in Houston, what might have seemed just a wild idea was eminently possible: Cullen/Frost had the opportunity to trade its Dallas operation for the two Corpus Christi offices of TCB.

According to Texas Commerce's president at the time, Mike Carrell, the bank was in no trouble. But it ranked only fifth or sixth in the Coastal Bend market: an awkward position which could only be improved by acquiring other banks there. TCB's parent corporation's goal was to compete as a star player in a prosperous market, studded with corporate headquarters, like Dallas, where it owned banks and had a substantial presence already. For both sides, the opportunity was sterling. At a special meeting in August 1993, the Cullen/Frost Board passed a motion to approve the swap. It also voted to merge the Cullen Center Bank and Trust of Houston into Frost Bank and to convert all three Cullen offices in the Bayou City to Frost branches. Thirdly, it elected several top officers to new positions of management, restructuring its operation.

That meeting would go down as one of the Board's most consequential of the decade. The upshot was that the corporation not only brought to bear the greater asset size of Frost Bank in Houston and solved its nettlesome Dallas problem but vaulted itself (with five offices) to the Number Three slot in the Coastal Bend market. It also moved $165 million in assets to its Corpus Christi base and boosted trust assets there to a robust $424 million. The downtown office's trust bounty, says Carrell, was soon to become the richest in the Coastal Bend area.

The reorganizational changes accommodated the new acquisitions and supported the new market focus. As Cullen/Frost was restructured into two principal divisions—Banking and Administrative Support— Frost Jr. became senior Board chairman of Frost National Bank. He remained Board chairman and CEO of Cullen/Frost Bankers Inc. But Dick Evans replaced him as Frost National Bank Board chairman. Evans was also named chief banking officer of the corporation, with responsibility for all banking offices statewide.

Meanwhile, Pat Frost, formerly top gun in the Retail Division, became the first fifth-generation Frost to become Frost Bank president, replacing Evans. J. Gordon Muir Jr. rose to the post of Cullen/Frost vice-chairman. Dave Beck became president of the Cullen Center bank in Houston. Huthnance officially took over the Austin operation; Mike Carrell would head things up in Corpus Christi; and Robert S. McClane, the perennial staff and operations guru, remained president of the holding company. These personnel moves were not cursory but strategic. They signaled the bank's return to a "stable-growth" from a crisis or "turnaround" mode by reshuffling the deck of existing officers without new face cards popping up. The bell of Frost tradition chimed again.

Another expansionary move had been the February 1993 opening (featuring a ribbon-cutting of old-style U. S. $100 bills) of a Frost branch near San Antonio's McCreless Mall. McCreless was not only the first new office the bank had opened in the city in five years but the first ever on the South Side. It occurred just as that less affluent part of town was rousing itself from economic torpor and making things happen; not coincidentally, the groundbreaking had taken place the day after a ceremony launching a new medical facility for Southeast Baptist Hospital—a South Side project in which Frost Bank had played a major role.

One month before that groundbreaking—in October 1992—history was made when U. S. President George Bush, Canadian Prime Minister Brian Mulroney, and Mexican President Carlos Salinas de Gortari initialed the North American Free Trade Agreement, or NAFTA. Despite opposition from some American diehards in 1993, NAFTA would become official (during the first administration of President Bill Clinton) on January 1, 1994.

NAFTA was crucial to Frost Bank because it was crucial to Texas and especially to San Antonio. In dollar volume, Mexico was America's second largest economic partner; trade along the border was growing faster than with its Number One partner, Canada. The accord would dramatically increase jobs in the Lone Star State for years to come. Even before NAFTA, Texas had been the leading exporter of goods to Mexico, accounting for almost half the total in 1991.

And San Antonio, of course, was the ideal hub for U. S. trade with Mexico. Of the $60 billion in commerce between the countries in 1993, $20 million was to flow through San Antonio and South Texas. Some 200 San Antonio-based companies—accounting for 65,000 jobs—did business on a large scale in Mexico that year. And 1.2 million Mexican visitors were spending $500 million in the Alamo City every year. As Mr. Joe predicted in the Thirties, Mexico had become a powerful economic generator for the city. What was good for San Antonio was good for Frost Bank and vice-versa. Mr. Joe's policy of cultivating relationships with Mexican banks, elevated to a Frost tradition, now seemed inspired. With ties to 16 of Mexico's 18 banks, Cullen/Frost was perfectly positioned to support cross-border trade and investment.

To flash forward a moment, bank and city lobbying for NAFTA, with Tom Frost Jr. at the forefront, would pay dividends in the March 1994 presidential decision to locate NAFTA's North American Development Bank, or "NADBank"—a bilateral vehicle to finance $3 billion in environmental and infrastructure work along the border, and a major financing vehicle for future trade between the U. S. and Mexico—in the Alamo City. Again, the whole world would hear about San Antonio. The NADBank drama is reenacted further on.

✦ ✦ ✦

Nineteen-ninety-three saw Frost Bank designated a certified lender by the Small Business Administration (SBA). SBA-guaranteed loans, the bank knew, were good business. They provided a wide, new range of methods to assist customers who could qualify; they allowed flexibility on collateral for fledgling companies; cash was not always required as security. Benefits to start-up entrepreneurs—Frost target customers by tradition—allowed them not only to secure a loan with less equity than on a straight bank loan but sometimes to negotiate a longer term.

Offering small businesses a helping hand had been Frost policy since the days of Colonel T. C. Frost. The expectation, fulfilled as often as not, was that these businesspeople would become successful entrepreneurs and want the bank that had helped create their fortune to remain the bank of their personal and professional assets all their lives. Entrepreneurs, Frost knew, tended to do all their business—from payroll to foreign currency exchange—with a single bank. It simplified things, and saved them time and hassles.

"By definition," says Bernard Gonzales of the Frost Community Reinvestment Act (CRA) Department, "a small business loan is any loan under a million dollars to a company with revenues of under a million dollars. The current Frost denial rate for small business loans is substantially less than the national average for banks, even community banks. We are a very active SBA lender."

As an example, Gonzales cites statistical data documenting that in 1997 the bank made 1102 small business loans, of which 890 were for under $100,001; 97 between $100,001 and $250,000; and 115 between $250,001 and $1 million. Given the size of the Frost loan portfolio, those numbers constitute percentages above the national average. Granted, during the Nineties, CRA reform required financial institutions to report what percent of their loans was being made to small businesses. But even before that, the numbers indicate, the Frost push to make SBA loans had been accelerating every year—in the hope that with its help, small businesses would grow up to become big businesses.

✦ ✦ ✦

The bank's largest community—Texas—was flying high again. Incredibly, after the sledgehammer blows it absorbed in the Eighties, the state led the nation in 1993 new-job creation. Its economy had become richly diverse, with the strongest gains in the services sector (particularly tourism and health care) and high tech (especially biotechnology and computers). Texas itself had become high tech, and Austin was its Silicon Valley. Oil and gas now accounted for just 12 percent of the state economy. Investor confidence in Texas companies was back to 1980 levels. By January 1994, Texas was the second most populous state, behind California.

Nineteen-ninety-four was a banner year for the corporation too, with pre-tax income of $57.6 million, up 51 percent from 1993's $38.1 million. Even the wildest-eyed optimist had not expected such a windfall; late in the year, Cullen/Frost increased its cash dividend from $0.15 per share per quarter to $0.22.

Did the corporation continue to strike while the iron was hot? Yes—but carefully and strategically. That December, as a response to changing marketplace conditions, Cullen/Frost bought a Houston-headquartered asset-based lender, Creekwood Capital Corporation: not a bank but a stand-alone corporation with $24 million in assets. The pricetag? Just $5.1 million. Houston was not exactly a new location, but Creekwood expanded the corporation's product line and gave it a new dimension at a bargain cost. Cullen/Frost also signed agreements that year, formalized in 1995, to acquire (1) the three-office National Commerce Bank of Houston for $24.2 million and (2) two Comerica Bank, Texas, branches in San Antonio for just $1 million.

Also finalized in 1995 was the purchase of Valley Bancshares, Inc.—including its subsidiary, Valley National Bank, in McAllen, Texas—for $9.2 million. The acquisition trumpeted Cullen/Frost's entry into the state's vast, emerging Rio Grande Valley and reinforced its reputation and visibility in South Texas. Crucial turf was marked as this "community bank's" community got bigger and bigger.

For Frost Bank, the biggest event of 1994 was the March decision to locate NAFTA's "NADBank" in the Alamo City. Frost Jr., Mayor Nelson Wolff, and other prominent locals had lobbied for it ever since the initialing of NAFTA in an historic October 1992 ceremony at the old German American School on South Alamo Street. With vision and foresight, San Antonio had been the first American city officially to come out in support of NAFTA. The mayor, the City Council, the Greater and Hispanic Chambers of Commerce, the local banks, and other major businesses had joined forces to make sure NAFTA was not ambushed in the alley.

Tom Frost Jr. had a private as well as public motive for bringing NAFTA's prestigious bank to San Antonio: family tradition. His grandfather, T. C. Frost Jr., had been an incorporator of the Federal Reserve Bank of Dallas back in 1914. His great-uncle, Joseph Hardin Frost, not only served six years on the Dallas Federal Reserve Bank Board and three more as a Federal Reserve district advisory councilman but in 1927 got a branch of the Fed established in San Antonio. His father, Tom Frost III, sat from 1942 to 1947 on the board of the San Antonio branch of the Federal Reserve Bank of Dallas. And by 1994, Tom Frost Jr. himself had over 15 years of Federal Reserve experience, six of them (from 1988 through 1993) as a *director* of the Federal Reserve Bank in Dallas. Flashing forward, it might be added that Dick Evans, though not a Frost family member, was to serve as a director of the San Antonio branch of the Federal Reserve Bank of Dallas from 1996 through 1998. Also, at year-end 1998, the board of directors of the Federal Reserve Bank of Dallas appointed Evans as its representative on the Federal Advisory Council, effective January 1, 1999.

To land a federal government bank for the Alamo City in the

Nineties was to affirm the time-honored Frost relationship with the Fed and to further a proud Frost tradition. *San Antonio Express-News* Business Editor David Hendricks reported that Frost Jr. had been "plotting a strategy" in Washington to bag the NADBank for his hometown as early as November 17, 1993: the day before the House of Representatives ratified the NAFTA legislation. The banker, reported Hendricks, sat up in the House balcony the night of the vote until the legislation passed. The following day, his lanky frame could be seen ambling from the Capitol to the Senate office buildings, where he would lobby Texas Senator Kay Bailey Hutchison about locating the NADBank in San Antonio.

The banker was determined to use every Washington contact at his disposal. That day also, he led a six-person delegation to the office of Treasury Secretary (and former Texas Senator) Lloyd Bentsen, offering rent-free office facilities for any NAFTA institution, including the NADBank. "I was there because Nelson [Wolff] had asked me to bring NAFTA institutions to San Antonio," Frost Jr. confirms. "Before I was through, I contacted approximately seventy-six individuals in San Antonio government, Mexican government, trade associations, the U. S. Congress, and the White House itself."

The lobbying paid off on March 25, 1994. During a flight to Dallas that day with Lloyd Bentsen, President Clinton informed his Secretary of the Treasury that he had decided on San Antonio for the NADBank. Bentsen wasted no time telephoning Texas Governor Ann Richards, who in turn phoned Mayor Wolff and directed him to call a press conference in San Antonio and announce the decision "before anything happens to change it."

San Antonio received 90 percent of the NADBank operation (including the headquarters), Los Angeles the other 10 percent. But also in downtown San Antonio—consolidated with the NADBank headquarters in a renovated former public library building at North St. Mary's and Commerce Streets—would be the offices of

(1) the Free Trade Alliance San Antonio, of which Frost Jr. was

executive committee chairman: a concentration of efforts by the city, the Hispanic and Greater Chambers of Commerce, and the EDF to make San Antonio a hub of international trade;

(2) an International Center, to bring together the major NAFTA trade alliances and individual entities engaged in international commerce; and

(3) CASAS (Spanish for "houses" or "homes")—an agency comprised of various houses of commerce financed by the states of Mexico to develop American exports and attract American investment.

The NADBank would be capitalized equally by the United States and Mexican governments; $3 billion would be authorized—and made available by the two governments equally—should the bank require additional capital; according to *The Wall Street Journal*, the system was modeled after the London-based European Bank for Reconstruction and Development, created to assist the former East Bloc nations after the Cold War.

Landing the NADBank was a brightly colored feather in the San Antonio community cap. Creating a vehicle to clean up and finance infrastructure along the polluted border had been crusaded for decades earlier by U. S. Representative Henry B. Gonzalez. Commented George Baker, a Mexico scholar at the University of California at Berkeley, "Placing the bank in San Antonio is good news. San Antonio has shown more than any other American city a sensitivity to its Mexican ties past and present. The decision to locate the bank there is a recognition of efforts over the last two decades to make San Antonio a cultural and historical bridge to Mexico."

On the day it happened, Frost Jr. told the media that a San Antonio-based NADBank would acquaint the world with "a place where major decisions are going to be made. That will attract people from all around the world to consider San Antonio the place to do business with Mexico." As with HemisFair and the South Texas Medical Center, the bank had fought and won a battle to put San Antonio on the map of the world's major communities.

The versatile and mobile Cullen/Frost vice-chairman J. Gordon Muir Jr., formerly chairman of the Houston Cullen bank, announced his retirement in 1995. The following year, another four-star officer, holding company President Robert S. McClane, would announce his. Muir went on to run his own bank elsewhere, while McClane became president of an outside company but continued to serve on the Cullen/Frost and Frost National Bank boards.

Nineteen-ninety-five saw a year of promotions that amounted to a personnel shakeup with the cast of characters, as was traditional, remaining the same. The constantly active Richard W. Evans Jr. replaced Tom Frost Jr. as Cullen/Frost Board chairman when the latter was elected senior Board chairman. Evans also became chief operations officer (COO), while Frost Jr. remained CEO. Executive Vice-President Phillip D. Green, who had served as Cullen/Frost treasurer since 1985, became the corporation's first chief financial officer (CFO).

Green's promotion, which increased his responsibilities far beyond those he had shouldered as treasurer, signaled the larger role he would play in the corporation's future: Now he would be in charge of (1) acquisitions, (2) investor relations, (3) finance and accounting functions, (4) an Investment Division for the bank-owned $2.1 billion securities portfolio, (5) operations and information technology, (6) property management, and (7) the bank's new data warehouse. That seven-part job description highlighted areas of crucial import for the bank in the forthcoming century. Perhaps the most exciting was the data warehouse itself.

Frost would begin building its futuristic data warehouse the following year, 1996, to provide analysis and decision support systems. Ultimately, however, the warehouse would accomplish much more. Board Chairman Evans said of it in 1995, "This warehouse will utilize a fantastic system that takes every single piece of data we have and analyzes it so we can know more about our day-to-day business. That will enable us to make more decisions based on our customers' needs." The system was to function, among other ways, like a customer questionnaire. How often do Frost customers use the ATMs? How about this or that Frost financial management service? Do customers increasingly borrow this kind of money or that? How often do they use the suburban branches as compared to the downtown banks? Such information, updated constantly, would prove invaluable.

With its completed data warehouse, the bank will also take giant strides in customer profitability analysis. Information will be used not just for more targeted marketing efforts but for detection of fraud, potential customer defection, and the tracking of customer buying trends. "It may take us years to perfect the system," Evans said. "But it will prove very profitable for us in the long run."

✦ ✦ ✦

As the world turned, the bank not only turned with it but kept its foot on a momentum accelerator. Slowly, the grim ordeal of the Eighties receded in memory. Its lessons, however, were not forgotten.

With 1995 pre-tax income of $71.3 million and a $46.3 million net income, the corporation saw its total assets break the $4 billion barrier. Noninterest income soared, with a remarkable correspondent-bank cash letter-processing operation alone generating $6 million in revenue. Cullen/Frost's office count rose to 46 as expansion escalated. Agreements, finalized in February 1996, were reached to acquire the five locations of Houston's Park National Bank (for $33.5 million) and to open new offices (on Stewart Road) in Galveston and in the Post Oak area (near the Galleria) of Houston. Those additions boosted total offices in the Houston/Galveston area to 14, up from just four a year earlier. The Oil Patch was back, but now it produced a lot more than oil.

Strategically, the Houston expansions enlarged the bank's presence westward from downtown into higher-income suburban areas.

Park National's assets were a resounding $249 million. "That bank was not only doing very well," says Houston/Galveston Regional President Dave Beck, "but it was also gifted with an extraordinary staff. It gave us better market share and dramatically enlarged our presence in the suburbs."

A brand-new market was opened in 1995 with the corporation's entry into San Marcos, Texas, along Interstate Highway 35, which connects San Antonio to Austin. Cullen/Frost signed a definitive agreement to purchase S.B.T. Bancshares, Inc. and its three-location, $112 million-deposit State Bank and Trust Company, San Marcos's largest bank. Finalized in January 1996, the buy gave the corporation top market share in a city that had posted an incredible 29 percent population growth from 1990 to 1995: almost triple the state average. The pricetag was an eminently reasonable $17.7 million.

The strategy was clear: Cullen/Frost was expanding not just into big cities but into fast-growing smaller ones that were part of major metropolitan areas. The corporation's eye was ever to the future.

Top row, left to right: Roy H. Cullen, a key negotiator of the historic "7-7-77" merger; Harry H. Cullen, another maker of 7-7-77 history; Isaac Arnold Jr., rounding out the trio of 7-7-77 Cullen family members on the Cullen/Frost Board. Below, left to right: Beverly Rust, chairman of the Trust Committee from 1969 to 1977, an era of prodigious Trust Department growth; United States National Bank building, Galveston's tallest when completed in 1925 and still a hub of activity.

*Clockwise from top left: Harris L. ("Bush") Kempner (1903-1987), a chief nego-
tiator in the 1982 merger of Galveston's United States National Bank with
Cullen/Frost; Harris L. ("Shrub") Kempner Jr., Bush Kempner's son, a Cullen/
Frost Board director; Austin's Chase National Bank (later Frost Bank North
Austin) was in 1982 Cullen/Frost's first expansion into the Austin market.*

Clockwise from top left: Retired Board of Directors Vice-Chairman Clyde Crews gave 30 years of stalwart service; Corporate Counsel Stan McCormick, secretary to the Cullen/Frost Board as of 1999; San Antonio River entrance to Rivercenter Mall.

169

This page, top to bottom: C. J. Krause being congratulated by Richard W. Evans Jr. on his 50th anniversary of Frost Bank service; Evans, Robert S. McClane, and Tom Frost Jr., left to right, celebrating the bank's 125th birthday in 1993 with a banker's birthday cake. Opposite page, top to bottom: February 1993 grand opening of the bank's McCreless branch, the first ever on the San Antonio South Side; International Center, housing the prestigious NADBank (which San Antonio landed with Frost help in 1994), at North St. Mary's and Commerce Streets.

171

This page, top to bottom: Very first stock certificates issued by Frost National Bank (1899); FrostBank Corporation (1973); Cullen/Frost Bankers, Inc., as Nasdaq member (1977); and Cullen/Frost Bankers, Inc., as NYSE member (1997). Opposite page, clockwise from top: Dick Evans, Tom Frost Jr., Patrick Frost, CFO Phillip D. Green, and New York Stock Exchange President William R. Johnston, left to right, at NYSE headquarters in August 1997, celebrating Cullen/Frost's listing on the Big Board and ticker symbol change to CFR. Patrick B. Frost, current bank president and youngest of the four Frost sons. Current Board Chairman and CEO Richard W. Evans Jr.

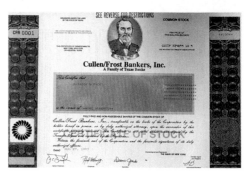

173

This page, top to bottom: Exploring an Overton Bank vault in Fort Worth are Dick Evans, center, with North Texas Regional President David L. Tapp, left, and Overton Bank and Trust Board Chairman Denny Alexander, right. Senior Board Chairman Tom Frost Jr. in 1998 is soon to embark on his seventh decade of service. Opposite page, top to bottom: Tom Frost Jr., seated, with sons Pat, Bill, Tom V, and Don, left to right, in 1999. Mr. and Mrs. Tom Frost Jr. with Mexican Ambassador Jesus Reyes-Heroles, right, at a November 1999 ceremony awarding the banker the highest honor Mexico confers on a foreigner–the Order of the Aztec Eagle Award.

174

175

chapter 11

Marching Toward the Millennium: 1997-1998

There was further expansion in 1997. That March, Cullen/Frost announced it would purchase Corpus Christi Bancshares, Inc., including its Corpus Christi subsidiary Citizens State Bank (assets: $211 million), for $32.2 million. A deft acquisition, it increased the total of Cullen/Frost offices to 52 and garnered the Number Two market niche in the Coastal Bend area, behind mighty NationsBank. "It brings us up to almost half a billion dollars' assets in the Corpus market," said Dick Evans, the corporation's Board chairman since 1995. "Call it a big step in our South Texas strategy."

"We did it," Corpus Christi Regional President Mike Carrell amplifies today, "because we wanted a substantially bigger presence in the Corpus community. We were about to buy a piece of land on the south side and build a new bank from scratch. But when we saw the chance to buy Citizens State, we jumped at it. With its six locations, that bank gave us coverage in every part of the city. It gave us a Calallen location, and later we added a Padre Island office. That positioned Frost banks all over the area, but especially southward, where real growth was occurring. And we already had a bank in nearby Portland." The Frost presence, in other words, had saturated the city.

Plans were also advanced for a second Frost location in McAllen, this one near the city's medical center, to open in mid-1997. The corporation meant to blaze a trail in the Rio Grande Valley—an area which, with its proximity to Mexico, fast-growing *maquiladora* business, and the passage of NAFTA, would become economically crucial in the century ahead.

It did not escape Frost notice that these acquisitions and expansions were costing a lot of money. In February 1997, Frost issued $100 million in capital securities to support its cash-backed acquistion programs. As a demonstration of how dramatically economic conditions had changed since the Eighties, investors actually lined up to avail themselves of the offer. The acquisition programs received all the support they needed. It was a significant victory: a vote of confidence from the public. As an added bonus, for the first time in their histories, Frost Bank and its holding company received investment-grade ratings from both Standard & Poor's and Moody's ratings agencies.

The corporation was spending a lot of money, but now it had the wherewithal to blaze trails again. Nineteen-ninety-six had been another banner year, with $54.978 million in net income. Total assets had risen to $4.9 billion, and trust income was up by $2.3 million, or 7.1 percent, largely thanks to higher personal trust fees. The rise in trust income was remarkable given the fact that Cullen/Frost had sold its corporate trust assets—between $4 billion and $5 billion worth—in May of the previous year, 1995. Its traditional, or personal, trust business had simply kept on booming.

Nineteen-ninety-seven marked a turning point for Frost's Trust Division and its investment functions when they were collectively renamed the Frost Financial Management Group. Richard Kardys, who had run the Trust Division, became the Group's first head. This new designation reflected the increasing importance of financial management to the company: As trusts were vital to its customers, so, increasingly, were the diverse investment services offered. The bold reorganization consolidated (1) private or "personal" trust services, including personal assets management, (2) financial management services, including managed accounts and brokerage activity, and (3) retirement services, including corporate 401(k)s, ESOPs, and KEOGH pension plans.

The Frost Financial Management Group was soon to become the nation's 56th largest bank trust division, approaching $12 billion in financial management assets. But Kardys and Executive Vice-President Jeanie Wyatt, who heads up the Investment Services component of the Frost Financial Management Group, contend that bigness was not the objective; catering to customer wants and needs was. Said Kardys, "Our bank had learned that customers *liked* to have all their eggs—banking, trust, and investment relationships—in one basket. The whole bundle was not only greater than the sum of its individual parts but worked more efficiently."

Throughout 1997, company history was made repeatedly as Cullen/Frost began its march toward the Millennium. Records were broken. Net income—$63.485 million—was the corporation's highest ever. Ditto total assets, which surpassed $5 billion. In the third quarter, 20 years after its first Nasdaq listing, Cullen/Frost began trading on the Big Board, the New York Stock Exchange (NYSE). It also changed its ticker symbol from CFBI, the old designation, to CFR.

Not only were prestige and credibility enhanced on the NYSE, but the company increased the liquidity of its stock through the Big Board's greater visibility. Also, transaction costs for investors were lowered, since the spread—or difference between the "ask" and "bid" prices—was $0.21

on the NYSE and $0.47 on the Nasdaq. Frost Bank President Patrick Frost made the first NYSE purchase—for 100 shares at 44 3/4—at 9:30 on the morning of August 14, 1997, the earliest available trading date.

Mysteriously, by this time, the price of Cullen/Frost stock had skyrocketed into the mid-40s from 1996's closing 33.02. Why? Surely, the move to the Big Board had not impacted liquidity *that* much. One plausible reason was that not until now was the public convinced Cullen/Frost had fully restored itself to its former viability and reliability. An even more plausible reason was that during this period, the bank stock index in general had soared.

In the fall of 1997, still making company history, Frost Bank entered its 11th Texas city when it opened a new branch in New Braunfels. Having entered San Marcos the year before, the bank now operated two offices along the vital business corridor of Interstate Highway 35 linking Austin to San Antonio.

History was more dramatically made that fourth quarter with the transition of the chief executive officer post from Frost Jr. to Richard W. Evans Jr., while the former remained senior Board chairman. Tom Frost Jr. admitted to being the first Frost ever voluntarily and officially to relinquish the CEO reins. "Of course, in the old days we didn't have a CEO per se," he qualified. "But there was always someone running the show."

The transition was remarkably smooth as the first non-Frost family member, or "outsider," began serving as the corporation's Board chairman *and* CEO. Certainly it was unprecedented. Was it also a preview of future power succession? Was Mr. Joe's "tight show" loosening up at last? Not necessarily. Evans's CEO appointment was a natural extension of his being named chief operating officer (COO) two years earlier. Frost Jr. and Evans had been working together on key bank issues and decisions for quite a while. Now both of them assured the press that the change was no significant departure from either Frost tradition or the way they had been running the bank for several years.

"Continuity of management has been a gradual process practiced through the generations by this institution," Frost Jr. stated. "My father gradually increased my duties and responsibilities over an extended period. What is occurring now is simply a seamless and orderly transition with a management team which, in accordance with our tradition, has grown and developed from within." An accompanying statement from Evans read, "This transition is in keeping with historical precedent at our bank. Tom Frost [Jr.] will still be at the bank, and we will continue to have access to his thinking, his values, and his enormous energy." It was important for the financial community and its analysts, not just depositors and shareholders, to perceive that the succession had been orderly; that the "Big Man" was still about; that Frost tradition had not been violated or Frost continuity disrupted.

As 1998 approached, there was even more change in the wind. Another, more dramatic change than a non-Frost's ascension as CEO was the restructuring of the sprawling, diverse, increasingly heterogeneous Frost market into five regions, each with its own president. Regional presidents would be empowered with responsibilities, authority, and decision-making autonomy unprecedented in the bank's history. Company offices would no longer be called banks or branches but "financial centers."

Though patently revolutionary, the move was also traditional and familiar, extending the Frost continuum. Just as Tom Frost III had decentralized management at Frost Bank in the Fifties by instituting departments, so Frost management was now decentralizing power in its far-flung markets by instituting regions and regional heads. Just as he had empowered officers at the bank with unprecedented authority and responsibility, so now were the regional presidents empowered. More and more decisions would be made at the market level, where contact with the customer was up-close and personal.

Four of the five regions, obviously, would be Austin, Corpus Christi, Houston/Galveston, and San Antonio, presided over by Robert T. Huthnance, Mike Carrell, Dave Beck, and Patrick Frost respectively.

The fifth, North Texas, would officially take shape the following year, 1998, with the Overton Bancshares expansion, which is recorded further ahead in this book. With it, the corporation would re-enter the Dallas market but also enter a new one: Fort Worth. The North Texas regional president would be former Overton Bank and Trust CEO David L. Tapp.

Why decentralize into markets and regions? There were many sound reasons, but the foremost, as usual, was relationship banking. Said Evans, "We base our marketing on customer values. Our marketing research tells us customers want relationship banking. The twenty to thirty megabanks offer a broad range of products and services but a very narrow process, and don't deviate from it much. The three to four thousand smaller, independent, community banks have a wide process—sometimes their relationship banking is conducted in one room—but limited products and services. We will offer the best of both worlds, since we're the only bank that can be big in capacity and small in process at the same time."

San Antonio Regional President Patrick Frost stated, "Our decision to decentralize was made to drive decision-making to local bankers in all our communities and bring us closer to our customers in those communities. The combination of strong relationships and a broad range of services will enable us to compete successfully with the megabanks."

Evans then added, "We only decentralized our organization one step further. We were already aligned into cities and areas. So we took each city or area and pushed responsibility and authority for it down another notch. The immediate objective was to empower a team closer to the customer—to operate as a series of community banks while still maintaining consistent quality and efficiency. That gave the individual bank officer the exciting chance to grow and develop in the way an entrepreneur does. But the ultimate objective was to remain competitive in a fast-changing, highly competitive industry. Our flexible Frost philosophy makes those kinds of adjustments possible."

But why start calling Cullen/Frost offices "financial centers" rather than banks or branches? The reason is self-evident: They had become more than just banks or bank branches. Indeed, they had become vehicles for personal investment and financial management. And soon, as Frost continued to turn with the world, they might even become vehicles for investment banking and the selling of insurance, activities previewed further on in this history. No longer just banks, they were literal financial centers, each individually devoted to the community it served.

Frost history was also being made with the unveiling of new products and services. The newly created agency Frost Leasing, for example, would build a superhighway of bank-assisted leasing opportunity for business customers throughout the state. And earlier, between 1995 and 1997, it had become possible for Frost customers to pay their bills "on-line" with their PCs or Macintosh computers at any time of the day or night. "On-line" and "home" banking instantly caught on, as had telephone banking with a trademarked Frost mechanism called the Touchtone BillPay. Another favorite with customers was a simple audio process—the Voice Response Unit—by which their phone call directed the bank to deduct from their account whatever they owed on a bill and remit it as designated.

Most exciting of all, the 1997 annual report promised that "Banking over the Internet will soon be available." Combining state-of-the-art technology with relationship banking, the report predicted, would "make the difference between banks that merely survived and those that prospered." Frost Bank had correctly made the same prediction in 1963, when it installed its first computer, an IBM 1401.

As 1998 dawned and the bank aproached its 130th birthday, it was time to expand in Houston again. How the Bayou City was booming!

Never had a town been driven so low, then risen up so fast. The nation's fourth largest city again boasted one of its highest employment-growth rates. Reliant on oil and gas no longer, it grew like crabgrass in computer production, international trade, and health care. Even its beleaguered petrochemical industry was pumping dollars again.

On January 2, 1998, the corporation put the final touches to its announced acquisition of Houston's Harrisburg Bancshares, Inc.: a middle-market commercial banking enterprise with three Bayou City area locations. This move implemented Frost's new niche strategy of providing middle-market commercial banking services. Just as important, it gave Frost a total of 18 Houston locations, the newer ones strategically located throughout the northwest and southwest sectors. At a cost of $55.3 million, it was the corporation's priciest acquisition to date. But it added assets of $265 million and established a presence in not just Harrisburg—near the Ship Channel and Port of Houston—but also the outlying suburban cities Clear Lake and Pearland.

Though a perfect fit for Cullen/Frost marketing strategies, the Harrisburg acquisition was the result of not calculated search but grasped opportunity and another family's integrity. The 73-year-old bank had been owned by the Harrisons, an oil-rich family highly respected in Houston. Tom Frost Jr. had met with them shortly after the Cullen/Frost merger in 1977 and asked the patriarch, Sam Harrison Sr., to consider Frost Bank should the Harrisons ever want to sell their own bank. The request was acknowledged, though no promise was made.

Twenty years later, in 1997, the younger generation of Harrisons finally was ready to sell. But they had another buyer in mind. Nevertheless, the patriarch's son Sam Harrison Jr. remembered the meeting, at which he had been present, between his father and Tom Frost Jr. He asked that Frost Bank be contacted before the deal went down.

That gesture bespoke volumes; the Harrisburg institution had maintained a correspondent bank relationship with Cullen/Frost, so Frost Jr. had known it was a class act, with many similarities to the Frost modus operandi. At the scheduled meeting, Frost made an offer, the Harrisons accepted it, and the deal was done. Again, serendipity and coincidence had oiled the motor of a Frost master plan. Again, "like had attracted like," with relationship banking the common ground. "With its focus on relationships and its strong community orientation," says Dave Beck, now president of the Houston/Galveston region, "Harrisburg Bancshares paralleled our way of doing business. And once again, we were able to buy a bank that was all but sold to someone else because of the respect people had for the Frost family and the Frost tradition."

Not only was Cullen/Frost growing by leaps and bounds but so was the price of expansion. Four months later, it would top its priciest-ever acquisition, the Harrisburg, with one that cost nearly five times as much but thrust it into a new market of immense strategic importance. In May 1998, it merged into the corporation Fort Worth's largest independent banking institution: Overton Bancshares, Inc. The price was a hefty $253.5 million, paid for with Cullen/Frost stock and marking the first time since the problem years of the Apocalyptic era that any purchase was financed in this way, all the others having been financed with cash.

Together with its subsidiary Overton Bank and Trust, Overton Bancshares specialized in middle-market corporate lending—a selling point for Frost—and trust services: another plus. It operated 12 offices in Tarrant County and two in Dallas. Being an $863 million bank holding company (with $1.8 billion in trust assets) gave Overton the sixth largest market share in the Fort Worth metropolitan region. The merger elevated Cullen/Frost assets to $6.6 billion; boosted its statewide deposit market rank from tenth to seventh; and increased its number of financial centers to 77 as the 14 Overton financial offices became what previously had been called Frost branches.

At first glance, the merger struck certain analysts as a strategic about-face, contrary as it was to the corporation's professed policy of steering clear of territories north of Austin—especially the Dallas market, which it had exited five years earlier. But when Evans termed it an "extension" of Cullen/Frost's Texas strategy rather than a revision of it, his terminology appeared to make sense. Clearly—particularly for a Texas bank, with the new century approaching—the vast Dallas/Fort Worth Metroplex was too prosperous a market to steer clear of. Overton's impressive numbers, nevertheless, were not an overriding motive for the merger. "Mergers," insists Frost Jr., "are not about numbers. They occur when we find people with the same philosophy of relationship banking as ours." For the fourth time in 20 years, Frost Bank had found such people. Actually, though, it had known these people for a good while, since Overton had been a Frost correspondent bank.

Merged this time was not some old downtown bank but a fairly new one, in a suburb: Fort Worth's Overton Park. It was a smart, conservative enterprise that managed to turn a profit every quarter of its operation during the Eighties. Said David L. Tapp, the Overton Bank and Trust CEO, "We feel as a group that our directors might be getting a little old, and that now might be the time to sell. With the current management structure remaining the same, we will continue to provide the personalized customer service for which our bank is known. We will also make credit decisions on a local level, since Frost and Overton share a community-oriented banking philosophy."

Frost-Overton discussions had begun on the weekend of the 1998 Super Bowl in January. In the bidding, Cullen/Frost beat out not only the finalist—fast-growing Compass Bancshares, Inc. of Birmingham, Alabama—but also four preliminary suitors. Now the corporation was back in Big D—though Dallas per se, having just two Overton offices, had not been a prime consideration. The bottom line was that an attractive new customer base had been laid in two of the state's three largest job markets—and near both Dallas/Fort Worth International and Alliance Airports.

Says North Texas Regional President David L. Tapp, "To date [December 1998] the merger has turned out at least as good, and probably better, than we expected. The Frost philosophy and values matched ours perfectly; thanks to such values, we'd both survived the Eighties. Our only surprises have been in areas where we thought we were actually doing a better job than Frost was. Mortgage banking, for example, is an area where they adopted *our* way of doing things."

Actually, the success of this merger should have come as a surprise to no one. Overton occupied a key position in the Fort Worth banking market. Like Frost, it was the customer-friendly homegrown bank, serving a goodly share of regional entrepreneurs who declined to cast their lot with those impersonal out-of-state megabanks suddenly dominant in their communities.

As Tapp implied, the merger also provided Frost an unusual opportunity to join forces with a management group whose relationship banking philosophies were remarkably similar to its own. This was reminiscent of the mergers with the Cullens in Houston and the Kempners in Galveston. At the same time, the merger attracted new investors seeking precisely the sort of relationship banking services Frost represented.

The fact that the transaction was negotiated for Cullen/Frost stock earned it substantial support from some of the most prestigious members of the Fort Worth community. With this merger, two extremely prominent Fort Worth businessmen, Overton Bancshares, Inc. Board Chairman Cass Edwards and Overton Bank and Trust Board Chairman Denny Alexander, became members of the Frost Bank and Cullen/Frost Boards. Frost's tradition of forging alliances with people of strong character and unimpeachable integrity, highly respected by their peers in their own communities, had prevailed again. That tradition is a proud hallmark in the growth and development of this quintessentially Texas banking organization.

In the fourth quarter of 1998, the corporation announced it would strengthen its new Tarrant County presence by acquiring the three offices of Keller State Bank (assets: $73.5 million) in a high-growth sector near Alliance Airport. The Keller purchase boosted the total of Cullen/Frost financial centers in Texas to the 80 mark. Once again, relationship banking had provided the muscle; as Keller State Bank Chairman and President Nick Theodore put it, "We are pleased to be joining an organization with a philosophy of customer service that closely parallels our own."

In October of that year, Frost Financial Accounting disclosed in a quarterly report that the corporation had earned a lusty $62.4 million during the first nine months of 1998. Loan volumes were up by 17.5 percent over those one year earlier. Recent acquisitions were paying off. No Texas community bank was as big or branched out as Cullen/Frost, with financial centers in San Antonio, Boerne, Austin, Corpus Christi, Dallas, Fort Worth, Galveston, Houston, McAllen, New Braunfels, and San Marcos. In Houston, the installation of Frost financial centers in the Exxon Building, St. Luke's Tower in the Texas Medical Center, and Kensington (for the former Sugar Land bank) gave the Bayou City 20 locations, two more than even San Antonio had.

At year-end 1998, Cullen/Frost employed a work force of 3204 people, larger than the population of many Texas towns. Such "bigness," however, was relative, and had not been a target goal. Though Cullen/Frost was the seventh largest bank holding company in Texas, it did not lose sight of the fact that six others were bigger. Even in San Antonio, its home field, Frost ranked but eighth in statewide assets among banks with branches there. The seven megabanks ahead of it owned 60 percent of such assets, and the top three (NationsBank, Chase Bank, and Bank One) held 45 percent all by themselves.

But so what? The bank was fulfilling its new mission, which was to stay close to customers and provide them with the personalized hands-on service those larger banks could not or would not provide. From that position, it could offer individualized banking solutions to the complex problems of small and mid-sized Texas businesses; only a community bank that genuinely knew and understood Texans could do that, even if the community was as big as Texas itself.

Community was the operative word, for banks are only as strong as the communities they serve. The community Frost served was strong again. Texas, the second most populous state, boasted 7 percent of the country's residents and employment base and 11 percent of its export market. (Were Texas a country, its economy would have been the eleventh largest in the world.) Austin enjoyed the state's fastest job-growth rate in high-tech and computer-related industries, where, a national news magazine reported, it had become one of the world's seven "nerve centers."

Meanwhile, Corpus Christi, with its deep-water channel and access to Mexico, was nationally noted for refining, chemicals, tourism, Gulf recreation, and other services; during the Nineties, the bank had nurtured its Corpus Christi community by financing projects like the three-ship Columbus Fleet replicas; the retired naval aircraft carrier *USS Lexington*; a "Touch of Frost" Christmas program, with the Corpus Christi Symphony; and an expansion of the charitable Ronald McDonald House. As the Millennium approached, the Frost tradition of giving back to its communities was alive and well.

New to communities like New Braunfels, San Marcos, and McAllen, Frost had not had enough time to make its nurturing presence felt. But one could bank on the certainty that it would. Its Houston, Fort Worth, and Dallas communities flourished again. Its native community, San Antonio, had come roaring back from its slump in the early Nineties, with Frost Bank its constant ally, to become one of the three fastest-growing communities in the state—the fastest in 1992—and the ninth largest city in America.

Big companies moving there accounted for such growth. Perhaps the biggest, Southwestern Bell Corp., or SBC—which relocated its corporate headquarters to San Antonio in 1992 after 113 years in St. Louis—disclosed that NAFTA and the growing interdependence of Texas and Mexico were factors in its decision. Another factor may have been Frost Bank. Tom Frost Jr. had sat on the board of Southwestern Bell Telephone Company from 1974 to 1983, and then continued to serve on the SBC (Southwestern Bell Corp.) board until 1998. The bank spared no effort in helping this prestigious Fortune 500 company relocate its personnel. The move brought 580 new jobs, most of them at the executive level, and a $30 million annual payroll. It meant a prominent downtown neighbor for Frost Bank and a prominent blue-chip company for downtown San Antonio.

The EDF was no less busy than Frost in luring attractive companies to the city. During the Nineties, this civic organization attained new heights of activism and success. From 1990 to 1998, it assisted over 100 major firms in moving to San Antonio, 18 of which created at least 500 jobs apiece, and seven of which—Boeing Aerospace Support Center, Worldcom, SBC Management Services, West Telemarketing Corp., QVC Network, Citicorp, and Teleservices Resources—created over 1000 jobs apiece. Another magnetic force, needless to say, in attracting new firms and jobs was the Greater San Antonio Chamber of Commerce, which was chaired in 1996 by Robert S. McClane.

Meanwhile, San Antonio's educational community was becoming major league. As Tom Frost Jr. served as chairman of the UTSA Downtown Advisory Committee, the summer of 1997 saw the opening of a long and badly needed UTSA branch downtown. Earlier, as chairman of the UTSA Development Board, Frost Jr. had involved the bank in raising capital for the university to offer doctoral degrees as part of a bold engineering/biosciences initiative; in 1993, as a result, UTSA created a Ph.D. program in biology, with an emphasis on neurobiology, and in 1995 a Ph.D. program in computer science. As of mid-1998, a doctoral program in electrical engineering was pending.

During the Nineties, individual efforts by Frost officers to further the cause of education in the Alamo City became even more vigorous. They were part and parcel of an old Frost tradition. Besides his development board involvements with UTSA, the University of Texas Health Science Center, and Our Lady of the Lake University, Tom Frost Jr. served on the board of governors of his old high school, TMI (Texas Military Institute). Don Frost, his second youngest son, was active on the board of prestigious old San Antonio Academy. Patrick Frost, his youngest son, was a member of the UTSA College of Business Advisory Council.

Outside the family, Robert S. McClane sat on the board at Trinity University. C. J. Krause is board chairman emeritus at Our Lady of the Lake University. Dick Evans is a member of both the United Negro College Fund Advisory Board and the Advisory Council of Executives for the School of Business Administration at St. Mary's University. The list is virtually endless.

Other Frost Bank community activity proliferated during the Nineties too. The Frost Progress Loan Program, initiated in 1991, was mentioned earlier, as were involvements in community job-training initiatives like Project Quest, on whose board of directors Tom Frost Jr. served as chairman. Tom Frost Jr. and Robert S. McClane continued in their determined effort, begun years earlier, to help address the chronic problems of the Edwards Aquifer (the city's primary water source) and to implement a broader-based water system. The bank also expanded its programs, begun in the Fifties, formalized in the Seventies, for keeping up-to-the-minute track of local employment indices. "If you run a bank in a city," went a Frost maxim, "you must understand how people in that city make their living. The most important service any bank provides is helping people earn a livelihood."

Helping people buy and maintain a home ranks a close second. According to CRA head Bernard Gonzales, Frost Bank received 390 applications for home purchase/home improvement loans in 1997 and approved 70 percent of them; the market average was 51 percent; the figures speak for themselves. And the 1998 introduction of home equi-ty lending in Texas finally gave the bank the opportunity to develop a significant line of business to customers theretofore not allowed to bor-row against the equity in their homes.

Even Texas weather summoned the bank to community financial support. Over the weekend of October 16, 1998, torrential rainfall and its flooding soaked much of what lay between Floresville and Austin, wreaking untold havoc. Eight flood-related deaths and losses of $115.7 million were reported in San Antonio. On October 19, Frost Bank an-nounced its donation of $100,000 to the American Red Cross for aid to its flood relief effort. Evans noted that New Braunfels, where Frost had most recently established a presence, was hit hardest by the deluge, fol-lowed by San Marcos, South Austin, and the bank headquarters: San Antonio. Again Frost Bank had put its money where its mouth was and given unstintingly to its communities.

By 1998, the decade had gifted the bank with a cornucopia of new technology. Frost "convenience banking" grew enormously popular. To open an account or apply for a loan, one needed just to pick up the phone. An automated telephone operation was soon handling 77 per-cent of Frost customer service calls: 339,000 per month.

In 1991, Frost's remarkable customized software, able to photo-graph 6000 checks per hour, then digitally record their images for monthly retrieval, had resulted in the bank's "Image Statement" mini-reproduction of 18 canceled checks on a single page, mailed monthly to Frost account holders. Similar to what American Express used for card-members, the technology saved time, drudgery, and postage. There were even environmental benefits: Since Frost customers wrote three million checks per month, paper checks could be recycled once their informa-tion had been stored to microfilm.

Frost's most exciting Nineties innovations lay in the realm of electronic banking. An electronic application process initiated in 1993 cut loan approval time to one business day. The following year, Frost became the first Texas bank to process a check by electronic transmit, allowing the paper check to remain at the originating bank and not have to be mailed to another. "On-line" convenience banking, mentioned earlier, caught on in a flash with personal computer (PC) owners. Banking via the Internet loomed on the 1999 horizon.

Most encouraging of all, exemplifying a Frost tradition when trouble approached, the bank launched a preemptive strike at the "Y2K" or "Millennium Bug" computer-scare nemesis in 1996, before most other banks did. Its June 30, 1998, quarterly report assured shareholders, "Our systems will be ready [for Y2K] well before the turn of the century. In fact, our core systems and mission-critical applications will be installed and tested by the end of 1998, allowing all of 1999 for certification." Taking note, a 1998 Salomon Smith Barney report rated Cullen/Frost as "one of the banks best prepared to handle the Y2K issue."

By January 2000, Cullen/Frost will have spent $4.5 million out of earnings to remedy Y2K glitches before they could occur. But that will prove $4.5 million well spent, since a run on banks was among the dread scenarios doomsayers had predicted and no price is too great to pay for depositor confidence. Seventy years earlier, that confidence had enabled the bank to survive a scare even greater than Y2K: the Great Depression of the 1930s.

✦ ✦ ✦

As Frost Bank celebrated its 130th birthday in 1998, its future looked bright. Its parent corporation was reaping profits from each of its 11 Texas markets and its 80 busy financial centers. Operating earnings for the year reached a record-high $85.2 million, up by a whopping 16.5 percent from 1997. For the fourth consecutive year, its cash dividend increased by at least 19 percent. And while the S&P 500 index was enjoying returns of just over 20 percent, Frost's largest internally managed stock fund was outperforming the S&P 500 with an amazing 12-month return of 32.4 percent.

Life was good. Elsewhere, with NAFTA and the NADBank in operation, the Frost International Department was expecting even more Mexican business in the forthcoming century. Going into 1998, Frost Bank's deposits from Mexico and its loans outstanding to Mexico (none of them nonperforming) were at an all-time high, as were trust fees from Mexican customers. Since its inception in the Fifties, when it consisted solely of Tom Frost Jr. and a secretary, the International Department had been buttressed by a succession of dedicated, hardworking officers like Hector Ortiz, Alicia de la Fosse, Earl Chumney, and Bernard Gonazles. At the century's end, that dedication was reaping its harvest.

"All those diversified opportunities in our Financial Management Group," Gonzales remarked in 1998, "plus the fact that now we do business with a younger, more sophisticated, better educated generation of Mexican nationals, are making our tradition of close ties to Mexico look better every day." Does Frost Bank plan to expand its offices into Mexico? Emphatically not, Gonzales insists. What sense would it make to create small-scale competition for all those Mexican banks it has a relationship with when they help to generate 80 percent of its Mexico-based assets?

Fortunately, in the late Nineties, as noncredit income from fees remained vital, the bank's trust operation continued to boom. In 1998, under the new banner of the Frost Financial Management Group, Frost's Trust Division reported almost $12 billion (counting the Overton and Galveston operations) in total assets as it managed three million gross mineral acres in 196 Texas counties and 17 other states.

Increasingly popular was the Financial Management Group's "Custody Account," which kept a custodian's watchful eye on customers' securities while allowing then independently to shape their investment strategies. The "Pathway to Prosperity" program, enabling middle-income investors (with at least $50,000 to invest) to avail themselves of the bank's expert financial-planning staff, was a success also. Meanwhile, Frost Brokerage Services, Inc. was saving investors commission-fee dollars while inviting them to trade by phone at any time during business hours.

Another exciting product on the Frost horizon, scheduled for announcement in 1999, was insurance—specifically life, accident, health, and property-casualty insurance. In 1998, with the striking down of laws forbidding banks to sell insurance, Frost Bank created the Frost Insurance Agency as a subsidiary, then began looking for a mid-sized Texas-based insurance agency as its vanguard into the state market. Such an agency, whose operating philosophy would be compatible with Frost's, could act as a hub for further Texas insurance agency acquisition. At year-end 1998, sources revealed that a suitable agency had been found and that a letter of intent to acquire it was being drafted. A few weeks earlier, Dick Evans had stated, "We know our customers, understand their needs, and feel there is a demand in the marketplace to add insurance to our business mix. Insurance is a natural extension of our bank's core personal and commercial banking as well as its financial management services. We are seeking an insurance provider that has already built a solid book of business in Texas."

With its commitment to providing quality insurance, Frost will offer customers a choice between purchasing their policies through the Frost Insurance Agency or directly from the bank itself. Such a choice goes to the heart of relationship banking: one-stop shopping convenience, interconnected services, personal contact with customers, and keeping a finger on the pulse of their ever-changing financial needs.

There was scarcely room on the Frost horizon at year-end 1998 for other new services. Yet one loomed as a solid possibility: investment banking.

By definition, an investment banker is one who, acting as underwriter or agent, serves as intermediary between an issuer of securities and the investing public. In December, according to company sources, Cullen/Frost was seeking Federal Reserve Bank approval to form a Section 20 investment banking subsidiary whose name would be Frost Securities. It was also talking to a duo of ex-Rauscher Pierce Refsnes (the former Texas investment banking firm) executives about heading up the subsidiary.

As so often, the strategy was both community- and relationship-driven: Frost wanted to give its commercial customers direct access to capital markets through a Texas-based organization. In the past, it courteously had referred them to out-of-state investment banks—and often lost them to those banks. Clearly, the potential for generating investment banking fees in Texas was huge; yet the fees were going to banks elsewhere. In 1997, according to Securities Data Company, firms in the Southwest with aggregate sales of under $2 billion generated an astronomic $156 billion in merger and acquisition transactions and $12.5 billion in the equity markets. That most of those firms reported 1997 revenues of less than $100 million positioned them squarely in the Cullen/Frost target market.

The new subsidiary would not only expand the range of services to existing customers but also develop a new customer base and leverage new relationships into Frost's commercial banking operation. Building the subsidiary from within rather than acquiring an existing company was less expensive, less risky, and ensured that it would grow within the parameters of the bank's traditional philosophy. It seemed a golden opportunity for Cullen/Frost, the largest independent bank in Texas, to become the state's premier independent investment bank as well.

✦ ✦ ✦

There was no glitzy gala celebrating Frost's 130th birthday in 1998, though one might have been in order were this conservative institution in the habit of publicly congratulating itself. Wracked by change, assailed by regional disaster, threatened with failure, and tested almost beyond endurance, it had weathered every storm of the previous 30 years like some indestructible old battleship. Now, for the time being, the sea was calm, the winds friendly. "What doesn't kill you makes you stronger," goes a philosophical adage—and 175 years ago, the celebrated English essayist William Hazlitt wrote, "Prosperity is a great teacher; adversity is a greater one." As it prepared to forge ahead into its third century of existence, Frost Bank, with an identity still as distinct as its founder's, had been made stronger by prosperity and adversity alike.

epilogue

The 21st Century

With an age of possible future shock at hand, a brand-new century and a new Millennium, how much change does Frost Bank anticipate for itself? The answer: very much—and very little.

That is a way of saying that this bank will change with the industry, and turn with the times, in matters of size, services, product, technology, method, and even communities, though expansion outside Texas should not occur. On the other hand, says Tom Frost Jr., "My vision is that we will *not* change the values and philosophy that have served us so well over the past hundred and thirty years. This bank doesn't have a history of radical policy change anyway. For all its growth, it's remained amazingly conservative, consistent, and moved forward incrementally: one careful step at a time."

His prediction bodes well for the bank's communities, particularly those newer, emerging ones, which should profit hugely from the nurturing Frost presence. A bank is, after all, not just a business but an institution: a word Webster defines as "a significant organization, like a college or university, within a society or culture." In 1866, the British statesman Benjamin Disraeli wrote, "Individualities may form communities, but it is institutions alone that can create a nation." Within the nation, however, a bank exists somewhere, not just anywhere, and that place is its community.

Making the community a better place to live renders it a better place to do business, and vice-versa. A good bank and a good community perpetually re-create each other. When it comes to Texas, many large, impersonal banks with their headquarters in other states have forgotten that; what makes Frost different—what makes it a community bank—is that it has not forgotten it. "Eighty percent of the biggest banks in Texas are no longer from Texas," a current television ad reminds us. "We're from here," says Frost Bank at the close of it.

With an identity as clear-cut as a person's, Frost Bank has not forgotten who it is. Nor has it put on airs and forgotten that it began in the corner of a one-room country store at a dusty crossroads. Like the store, it tried to serve those who would develop that crossroads into a community. From the start, the bank was both less than a bank and more: "less" because it ranked people above profits (which good business and hard work would make inevitable) and growing the community above lining its founder's pockets; but "more" because it took on the role of a community institution, like a school or church, whose first reason for being was the betterment of lives around it. That essential *raison d'etre* will not change.

Other kinds of change, however, comprise a Frost tradition and should continue at an even more accelerated pace in the century ahead. There will be more financial centers, more acquisitions and mergers, more expansions; one acquisition, that of Fort Worth's Bank of Commerce, is planned for 1999. And the Frost forays into uncharted territories of Internet banking, home equity lending, insurance, and investment banking will surely mean far-reaching change, with all sorts of new business, challenge, and excitement. For this bank, the 21st Century will begin with a bang.

Going in, business should be good. Though economic indicators point to a cooling of the currently overheated national economy—and a concomitant slowing down of the Texas economy—the long-term outlook is for sustained growth in key industrial sectors of the state. Texas should continue to prosper, as it has since the Eighties Apocalypse. Prior to that, oil and gas accounted for almost 20 percent of the Lone Star State's economy; today's figure, thanks to rapid diversification in the interim, is around 7 percent. With just 4 percent of today's Cullen/Frost loan portfolio oil-and-gas related, energy industry fluctuations are no longer a constant concern.

Frost Bank President Patrick Frost is optimistic about the future—though not blindly so. "I don't want to see us become less conservative," he stresses. "In a sense, we're going through a dangerous time now. Because these will be remembered as the 'good old days' of economic prosperity, lending standards are loosening, boundaries disappearing, and there's tremendous pressure to show quarterly earning increases once again. We may be witnessing a repeat of the early Eighties. But this time, we'll be ready." Forewarned, he implies, is forearmed.

With Pat Frost bank president and Don, Bill, and Tom Frost V in other executive positions, the tradition of Frost-family officers at the highest echelons will continue. But flexibility and adaptability are also Frost traditions, and nowadays—apart from that of the senior Board chairman, Tom Frost Jr.—considerable power is wielded by the team of the Board chairman and CEO, Richard W. Evans Jr. Windows of opportunity for Frosts and non-Frosts alike are wider than at any time in the bank's history. Yet continuity will be preserved; Frost Bank will be Frost Bank; the importance of such stability can scarcely be overemphasized. The fact that no one can predict who will be at the corporation's helm in, say, the year 2010 is interesting and exciting.

One *can* predict, however, that Frost Bank will still stress the

"Four Cs of relationship banking": credit, capital, collateral, and character. All abide as cardinal virtues, but at Frost the greatest of these is character. According to legend, the American financier J. P. Morgan, asked what he considered the best bank collateral, replied "Character!" "When you assess a customer," Mr. Joe exhorted in the Twenties, "get the facts about his character. That way, you avoid mistakes. Do business with people of good character; they have a track record of success; when they succeed, so will we."

His great-nephew Tom Frost Jr. tells the story of a loan applicant, sans capital and collateral, who sat in his office pleading for credit. "What about my character?" the applicant demanded. "I thought you made loans based on character."

"Character," the banker coolly responded, "is what got you into that chair. It's the beginning, not the end."

At Frost Bank, all the same, there remains a sense in which character is the end as well as the beginning. Much as anything, it is what has enabled this venerable old institution to survive runs, panics, recessions, depressions, world wars, Arab oil embargoes, energy disasters, real estate collapses, Eighties greed, and its own occasionally huge, foolish mistakes. By having not just endured but prevailed throughout its tempestuous 130-year history, Frost Bank has borne out the classic belief, old as antiquity and held by the Colonel, that character is destiny.

acknowledgments

Much information contained in this history is based on written documents. There were financial reports, board meeting minutes, statistical tables, market quotations, and press releases; there were published histories of the bank, the city, HemisFair, the South Texas Medical Center, the state banking industry, and the American nation; there were family chronicles of the Frosts, the Cullens, and the Kempners; there were newspaper articles and magazine articles, and there were well-preserved 19th Century letters and memos from the Frost National Bank archives. These and other documents served to construct the skeleton of this history.

Its bones were endowed with living flesh by oral history interviews with the *dramatis personae*—people who were not just there while Frost Bank history was being made but who actively made it. They imbued what might otherwise have been a drab, dispassionate, formal chronology with their warmth, wit, verve, and vivid recollections.

I am indebted to these interviewees, who are listed below. Either in person or by telephone, and often both, they contributed anywhere from 10 minutes to (in the case of Senior Board Chairman Tom Frost Jr.) over 40 hours of their valuable time fielding my questions. I only regret that I could not mention or quote them all.

Endlessly helpful to me were my invaluable Frost Bank liaison, Senior Vice-President Judy McCarter of the Marketing Department, as well as retired Frost Bank Senior Vice-President C. J. Krause, whose veteran service encompassed more yesteryears than that of anyone else contacted. Thanks and praise to both.

A footnote to the alphabetized list of interviewees below: The interview with the late Angelo Drossos occurred years ago, and for a different project; the subject, however—the role of Frost Bank in bringing the (currently NBA champion) San Antonio Spurs to our city and keeping them here—is as timely now as then. One could have hoped for no better source.

Tom Walker
June 30, 1999
San Antonio, Texas

Oral History Interviewees

Chip Allen

Karen J. Banks

David W. ("Dave") Beck Jr.

Mike Benson

Paul H. Bracher

Mike Carrell

Charles E. Cheever Jr.

Lila Cockrell

Clyde Crews

Roy H. Cullen

Kemper Diehl

John Donohue

Angelo Drossos

Carolyn Elliott

Richard W. ("Dick") Evans Jr.

R. E. ("Buster") Fawcett Jr.

David ("Dave") Finger

Lewis E. Fisher

Carlos Freymann

Donald B. ("Don") Frost

Patrick B. ("Pat") Frost

T. C. ("Tom") Frost Jr.

Tom Frost V ("Tom III")

William ("Bill") Frost

Bernard Gonzales

Phillip D. Green

James L. ("Jim") Hayne

David Hendricks

Robert T. Huthnance

Rabbi David Jacobson

Richard Kardys

Harris L. ("Shrub") Kempner Jr.

Patricia ("Pat") Konstam

C. J. Krause

Steve Lee

Robert S. McClane

Red McCombs

Stan McCormick

George C. Mead

Mrs. W. Oscar Neuhaus

F. A. ("Andy") Odom

Albert Price

Frank Sievers

William R. ("Bill") Sinkin

John Spencer

David J. Straus

David L. Tapp

Robert Vontur

Richard ("Dick") Votel

Jeanie Wyatt

index

Illustrations in this book are not indexed.